# THE CHARACTER COACH

A Guide to Making
Good Kids
Great

## Daniel Klapheke

Order this book online at www.trafford.com/07-0415
or email orders@trafford.com

Most Trafford titles are also available at major online book retailers.

Note for Librarians: A cataloguing record for this book is available from Library
and Archives Canada at www.collectionscanada.ca/amicus/index-e.html

Printed in Victoria, BC, Canada.

ISBN: 978-1-4251-2011-5

*We at Trafford believe that it is the responsibility of us all, as both individuals
and corporations, to make choices that are environmentally and socially sound.
You, in turn, are supporting this responsible conduct each time you purchase a
Trafford book, or make use of our publishing services. To find out how you are
helping, please visit www.trafford.com/responsiblepublishing.html*

*Our mission is to efficiently provide the world's finest, most comprehensive
book publishing service, enabling every author to experience success.
To find out how to publish your book, your way, and have it available
worldwide, visit us online at www.trafford.com/10510*

 www.trafford.com

**North America & international**
toll-free: 1 888 232 4444 (USA & Canada)
phone: 250 383 6864 ♦ fax: 250 383 6804 ♦ email: info@trafford.com

**The United Kingdom & Europe**
phone: +44 (0)1865 722 113 ♦ local rate: 0845 230 9601
facsimile: +44 (0)1865 722 868 ♦ email: info.uk@trafford.com

10 9 8 7 6 5 4 3 2

## DEDICATION

To my son, Aidan, who's my motivation to be the world's best
Character Coach.

To my loving and supportive parents, Bernadette and Harry
Klapheke, who certainly
don't need this book.

To my wife, Alisha, for putting up with me
and loving me.

# CONTENTS

## ACKNOWLEDGEMENTS

It would be nearly impossible to thank everyone who has come and gone in my life that has influenced and taught me. I owe all of my knowledge to so many people. The following is just a short list:

Thank you to my wonderful wife, Alisha, who not only supported and guided me, but also helped with the initial editing.
My parents for their love, guidance, and support.
My gracious editor, Pamela Jones.
All of my students and their parents for their inspiration and influence.
Thank you to all Character Coaches who are working hard to change the world.

Some stories provided in this book were passed down to me from my teachers or are old fables I picked up along the way. I wish I knew the origin of all of them so I can thank and credit them.

# PREFACE

## HAVE YOU MET THIS KID?

When he was 3 years old, he would scream until he got his way. He still sucked on his pacifier. He's the kid you'd see having a temper tantrum in the store because Mom wouldn't buy him a particular toy. She would give in and eventually buy it for him though. He's the kid who calls his Mom names and even slaps her. Mom's response? Whatever makes him happy. Whatever makes him shut up. When he really pushes her, she warns him that there will be consequences. She warns him and warns him and warns him, but never follows through. When he starts kindergarten, he's always in trouble because he has no self control. He can't sit still. He talks out of turn. He throws regular temper tantrums, and he certainly doesn't share with his classmates. In grade school, his grades are below average. He still talks too much. He doesn't complete his assignments. He acts up in class for attention. His teacher has to drag him to the principal's office for being out of line. He likes it though. He likes the attention. He knows that the principal and teachers aren't allowed to lay a finger on him. He thinks he can get away with anything. What are they going to threaten him with - the wrath of mom and dad? When he gets home from school everyday, he heads straight for the pantry for some fattening snacks and from there, to the television. He watches his favorite show and then plays his video games for a couple of hours. Next, he wants more junk food to eat. After throwing the wrappers on the floor next to the wrappers and cup from yesterday, he lays down on the couch. When his Mom asks if he has finished his homework, he says "yeah." He's lying. During dinner, he doesn't finish his food, and he doesn't clean up after himself. He's too busy for that. He has more video games to play and TV to watch. Does he go to bed on time? No way. Of course not.

Let's fast forward. Somehow he makes it to college. He spends most of his time partying and waking up at noon most days. His major is undecided. He just doesn't care. After five or six years, he eventually graduates and gets a job. It's a job far below even *his* standards. It doesn't pay well and the money he does make he wastes on junk. So he can buy even more junk, he gets a credit card and starts running that debt way up. Since he can't afford his lifestyle, he has to move in with Mom and Dad again. He doesn't do a thing around the house to earn his keep. He pays no rent and has no chores. Why should he? He's never had to be responsible before.

One day, he finally gets married. It's doomed from the start. He's still just as lazy. He is still just as undisciplined and he has no respect for anyone. He's verbally abusive to his wife. He still doesn't lift a finger around the house. He still digs deeper into debt. The marriage becomes so strained, he's soon divorced and working at minimum wage. His life is in ruins.

What is the real reason for his miserable life? Is it just bad luck? That's what most people would say. Most people in his shoes just think they've been dealt a bad hand. To some extent, they're right. But ultimately, everyone is responsible for their own decisions. Why didn't he make good decisions? Because his parents never held him responsible for his actions. Because he never learned to respect others. Because his parents failed him he's now doomed to failure. Being a success at anything starts with important life skills such as respect, discipline, self-control, responsibility, and integrity. Knowing what these traits mean is not enough. They must be learned through example and experience, and they must become so ingrained that they become habits. It is up to the Character Coach to teach and guide them. It's not up to the Character Coach to be their best friend or fulfill their every wish. The job of the Character Coach is to teach them boundaries and respect along with self-love that comes from loving others.

All of our kids will go through phases. No one is perfect. Your kids and mine will ultimately display some of these characteristics at some point or another. The kid in our example displayed bad habits and choices on a consistent basis. The point is to make sure this type of behavior never becomes a habit.

# INTRODUCTION

In 1985, my father introduced me to martial arts training and it was one of the best things that ever happened to me. My training helped me understand the importance of good character. I loved the martial arts so much that I became an instructor. For more than a decade, I have taught tens of thousands of children valuable life skills through the martial arts. Skills like goal setting, focus, discipline, self control, respect, and perseverance. For thousands of years, these fundamental principles of character have been part of the martial arts curriculum. The old Asian masters knew that they formed the foundation for a whole, healthy individual.

In the martial arts, if you don't behave in a certain way, you face a creative and memorable punishment. In the beginning of my training, I learned the importance of the Principles of a Black Belt because I was terrified of my instructor. Because of this fear, I always said, "Yes, sir," and paid close attention in class. I stood still and continually tried to do my best. Since then, martial arts training has changed. With the advent of commercial martial arts schools, the curriculum has become more kid friendly. Some old-school martial arts teachers still like to use the drill sergeant techniques to teach their trade. They feel like they need to scare their students to make them respect them. In my experience, this is not necessary.

At my martial arts school, we have a more updated approach to teaching children both the physical and mental skills of martial arts. Years of research and mentoring have taught me how to really get through to kids without resorting to scare tactics. I've seen some incredible changes in many kids over the years. I still get a real thrill out of molding kids into the best young people they can be. It happens from the inside out. They develop very effective karate skills, but it all begins with building character. Character will ultimately earn a Black Belt, improve their grades in school, help them advance in sports, and equip them to develop stronger and healthier relationships with their friends and family.

Raising a kid from white belt to Black Belt is not unlike raising a child from infancy to adulthood. A new student doesn't have a clue about proper behavior and protocol in a karate school. They obviously don't possess any physical martial arts skills. They can't handle a group class without some one-on-one attention first. Just like a baby, they need guidance and nurturing. They need to be taught about expectations from the very first day. A strong role model - a Character Coach - is absolutely critical in their youth and development. They need a confident person to pick them up when they fall. They need someone to steer them back when they are going the wrong way. A good martial arts instructor, coach, or teacher can shape the personality of a child in a positive way, just by working with him or her for an hour or two a week. Imagine the life-changing impact that a parent can have on their kids if they apply the same techniques on a consistent basis. This is the parents' job. Dave Ramsey, in his best selling *Financial Peace,* said it best when he stated: "Children who reach the age of eighteen with their entire skill set composed of Nintendo and Doritos have been abused. I am not speaking of child abuse in the sense of sexual or physical abuse, but neglect. The parents neglected the child by not giving him the character traits needed to live successfully."

Without strong characters, our young people are decaying socially. They are becoming more and more selfish, lazy, irresponsible, rude, violent, and in some cases, heartless. Zig Ziglar, in his book, *Raising Positive Kids in a Negative World*, paints a clear picture of where our society is headed when he writes: "According to Dr. Marvin Watson, former president of Dallas Baptist University, in 1940 the top offenses in public schools were as follows: running in hallways, chewing gum, wearing improper clothing (which included leaving a shirttail out), making noises, and not putting paper in wastebaskets.

Today the top offenses in public schools are as follows (not in order of occurrence): murder, rape, robbery, assault, personal theft burglary, drug abuse, arson, bombings, alcohol abuse, carrying weapons, absenteeism, vandalism, and extortion." If this doesn't scream PROBLEM! then I don't know what I can say to convince you. As a society, our values and morals are becoming more and more diluted. Too many parents are letting society raise their children. Television, radio, other kids' parents, teachers, instructors like me, police, you name it, are becoming the agents of child rearing. This hands-off approach to parenting isn't parenting. It's neglect. Parents and other Character Coaches have to take responsibility and turn this thing around. It all starts with you. It starts with dedicated, educated parents and role models.

This book will help you better understand the principles of success and how to convey them to children. Take your time and read the helpful guidelines on parenting and Character Coaching provided in the first section of the book. The second section covers the pillars on which good character is built. I offer insights and thought-provoking stories for introducing these pillars to your children. Following each story are follow-up questions that you can ask your child and a summary of the messages. The last section of the book deals with the final transformation of a child with a strong positive character into a young person armed with the principles they need to succeed in achieving their dreams.

## WHO IS THE CHARACTER COACH?

YOU! This book is for parents, teachers, instructors, counselors, coaches, and anyone else who works with children. Whether you are a parent or a professional role model, I will refer to you as The Character Coach. Much of the text is directed towards parents. When I refer to parents and offspring and you are not one or do not have any, just remember that your interest should be the same. "Your kids" may not actually be *your* kids, but if you work with kids, I am sure that you truly care about them. I treat all of the kids that I work with the same way I would treat my own.

## HOW TO USE THIS BOOK

Read each chapter carefully several times before you begin teaching your children the lesson. This will help ensure that you have a good understanding of the topic so you can teach it with confidence.

Each lesson includes a story that helps your child visualize the message you are trying to teach them. If they hear a story with a message in it, they are much more likely to remember, not only the story, but the point of the story too. You can also use the story as a reference point later. For example, if she is not being respectful, you can remind her by saying, "Remember what happened to Noah in the story about the Black Belt who didn't bow?"

Each story is followed up with questions you can ask to help ensure your child gets the point. When they hear themselves answer questions, it helps them learn on a deeper level. Have a discussion about each question. Really drive home the message you are trying to get across.

Remain enthusiastic. Be sure to make the learning process as fun as it can be. The more fun you make it, the longer children retain interest. Building a child's character takes a great deal of time and repetition, so you want to keep the child involved as long as possible. After you've covered all of the principles in this book, start over, and do them all again. Repetition is the mother of learning. Only cover a lesson or two per month. This will allow you to give the subject the proper attention. It also allows you and your child to focus on one principle at a time. Reiterate the covered lesson as much as possible in their daily life. If you are working on focus, then make sure you are constantly reminding them about focus. Ask them questions about focus such as: "Did you focus on your teacher today at school?" or "What is it called when you really concentrate on the bull's eye when you are shooting your bow and arrow?" Make the process important. If it is important to you, it will be important to them. After all, what is more important than your child's character?

Throughout this book, I share the insights I have developed through mentoring other parents and teachers, traveling to seminars, constant reading and studying, and ten plus years of teaching children at my own martial arts school as well as dozens of elementary and middle schools. I have a great passion for making positive changes in kids, and I can't wait to share it with you. So turn the page, and let's get started.

# PART I

BEING A
CHARACTER
COACH

# IT ALL STARTS WITH YOU

*"Who you are and the person you want your child to become has to be the same."*

**DANIEL KLAPHEKE**

Kids are like sponges. Since the world is still new to them they soak up everything they see and hear. A child spends more time with his or her parents than anyone else. Consequently, parents are the biggest and most important influence a child will ever have as author Dorothy Law Nolte observes in the title of her book "Children learn what they live." If kids see their parents yell at each other, they will become hostile. If Mom talks behind Dad's back, the kids will become deceitful. If Dad eats a huge dessert after most meals, the kids will over-eat junk food. If Mom loses her temper, the kids will become temperamental. The old adage, "Monkey See, Monkey Do," is true. As a Character Coach you have to be a monkey worth mimicking. So it's time to roll up your sleeves and be the best darn monkey that you can be! It's not easy. If being the perfect role model was simple, all parents would raise kids who were confident in their capabilities and kind to others. We all know that being a role model, a Character Coach, is a demanding, full-time job that requires hard work and hours of over-time. We all know parents who work harder at their day jobs than they do raising their kids. This is an easy trap to fall into—I'm doing it right now as I write this book. Of course, providing for your kids is very important, but we have to also make time to be a good parent. Kids have to be our priority, period. When you feel like you don't have time to play with or listen to your kids, remember this sobering thought: If you fail to give your kids the attention they need and deserve, they'll find someone else who will. And there's no assurance that person will be a positive influence. So, always make time for your kids.

Your children should always be at the top of your "to do" list. There's an old cliché, that makes an important point. "When you're on your death bed, you won't be wishing you had spent more time at the office." Instead, you'll be thinking about relationships, and the most important relationship, in my opinion, is the one with your kids. It seems like yesterday your child was in diapers, doesn't it? Time flies. Be sure to spend quality time with them before it slips away.

A child's character is formed by the decisions you guide them to make and the habits those actions create. Before we can generate positive habits in our children, we must first embrace those habits as our own. As you read this book, don't make the mistake of thinking these principles are just for your child. First and foremost, they are principles for your life. If you want to instill confidence and discipline in your kids, you must teach by example. Remember "Monkey See, Monkey Do." Notice the line doesn't say "Monkey Hear, Monkey Do." Kids learn from their parents' and role models' actions. There's another adage that says, "Your actions speak so loudly I can't hear what you are saying." In other words, you must be able to walk your talk. If you lack the characteristics you want your kids to learn, then start acquiring them now. It's not too late. Read personal development books, listen to audio books on the subject, and learn by observation. Until you have embraced the principles that follow in this book, I encourage you to at least fake it until you make it. As you work to improve yourself, at the very least pretend you are a person of strong positive character while your kids are around you until you actually possess these skills. If you "pretend" long enough, you will eventually become that someone. Be careful in the process. Kids are smart. They can see right through you if you do not "walk the talk." If you have to fake it for a while, do it well, and strive to become that person as fast as you can. The sooner you build more personal character, the sooner your child will follow in your footsteps. If you exhibit strong positive character traits, your child can't give you the old "But you do it, why can't I?" routine. It's not an easy process, but for the future of your family tree, start working on character building right now, today.

Read the following verse and recite it over and over. When being a good role model becomes challenging (and it will), say it to yourself, believe it, and apply it to living and parenting every single day.

**We sow our thoughts, and reap our actions.**
**We sow our actions, and reap our habits.**
**We sow our habits, and reap our characters.**
**We sow our characters, and reap our destiny.**
*Anonymous*

## POINTS TO REMEMBER

- It all begins with you.
- Make sure that the person you are is congruent with the person you want your children to become.
- You can't give something to someone that you don't already possess. This is especially true with character.
- "Do as I say, not as I do" is usually a cop-out.
- Be consistent.
- Be a good example.
- Follow through.

# CREATING GOOD HABITS

*"We first make our habits, and then our habits make us."*

JOHN DRYDEN
17TH CENTURY POET

Human behavior, good or bad, is shaped primarily by habits. Studies show that 95 percent of everything we do, think, and feel is out of habit. Habits can be good or bad, but they are powerful in deed. Saying "thank you" is a good habit. Belching out loud is a bad habit. Exercising on a daily basis is a good habit. Crashing on the couch when you get home from school is a bad habit. If you analyze your actions, you'll be amazed at how much you do out of habit. Do you know which shoe you put on first? Do you put your seat belt on before or after you start the car? The point is we do so much without having conscious knowledge of it. Habits control your behavior and your actions ultimately form your character. A habit is just a decision you make over and over again.

It feels like you can't help it when a habit takes over. Habits are hard to control and we all know it's tough to "break" bad habits. New habits sneak up on you from behind. It's like boiling a frog. If you drop a frog into boiling water, it will immediately jump out. But if you place the frog in room temperature water and slowly heat the water up, the frog won't notice the rising temperature until it's too late. Habits are sneaky too. If you repeat an action often enough, it will become a part of you. Research shows that repeating an action for 21 consecutive days can lead the action to become a habit. This includes both good habits and bad.

As Character Coaches, we must strive to nurture and create good habits while breaking our bad habits. Only then can we help guide our children to do the same. So successful Character Coaches should always exhibit good habits in their actions. Unsuccessful coaches do not. Decide on a habit or character trait you wish you possessed. Some people wish they could get up earlier in the morning or exercise on a consistent basis. These are things that you can actually program yourself to accomplish. Just make it a point to do them consistently for at least 21 days in a row. With a little effort and self discipline, you won't need to set the alarm clock in the morning to wake up early, and your body will need an exercise fix without you scheduling it. Start with something small and work your way up. The more success you have at acquiring good habits, the more success you'll have programming your children.

Your child's brain is like a computer. It is actually far more advanced than any computer will ever be. Like a computer, your child's brain needs programming, the kind achieved through good habits. Brian Tracy in "Million Dollar Habits" says: "For more than 100 years, psychologists have worked to understand and explain the functioning of the human mind. Starting with Sigmund Freud and continuing through Alfred Alder, Karl Jung, Abraham Maslow, William Glasser, Eric Fromm, and B.F. Skinner to the present day, psychologists have sought reasons for happiness and unhappiness, success and failure, achievement and underachievement. They have all concluded, in one way or another, how your mind is programmed in early childhood plays a decisive role in almost everything you think, feel, and accomplish as an adult." This is a powerful statement that shouldn't be taken lightly. Take a moment and think of the type of personality that you wish your kids would possess as adults. Then start helping your children form habits that will make them the best that they can be.

One of the most important habits anyone can possess is a positive mental attitude. Having a positive or negative attitude is a result of how your mind is programmed by your habits. If your child is a complainer and finds the negative in everything, catch that child as often as possible when he or she complains or says something less than upbeat. Remember it starts with you. If you're a complainer with a negative outlook, take steps to change now. However you handle life, your child will do the same. If you complain about the heat, how can you expect your child to handle the heat? Accentuating the positive or negative affects your child's feelings towards the situation. If your child thinks that it's terrible that it's raining because he can't skateboard, you have a recipe for a lousy day. It certainly won't help if you're griping too because you just washed your car. Instead, be happy about the rain, no matter what you planned for that day. Find the good in it. All of the plants outside need rain to grow. Rain puddles are fun to play in. The air after the rain is clean and clear. You can't find a rainbow on a sunny day. Remember that you might have to fake it until you make it sometimes, but it's worth it. You cannot raise positive kids if you're negative, and accomplishments start with a positive attitude.

Congratulate your child when he or she says positive things and correct that child gently when he or she makes negative comments. Before long, both of you will have more positive attitudes. We will discuss positive mental attitude more later, but start right away by accentuating the positive.

King Solomon himself saw the value in programming children with good habits. In Proverbs 22:6, he says: "Train a child in the way he should go and when he is old he will not depart from it." Keep this principle in mind as often as possible because this mindset will make this book work for you. All of the success principles we discuss must eventually become habits which will form your child's character and ultimately his or her destiny.

## Points to Remember

- As Character Coaches, we must first nurture good habits and break bad habits in ourselves. Only then can we guide our children to form good habits.

- The way we program children in early childhood plays a decisive role in almost everything they think, feel, and accomplish as adults.

- The habits that your child develops today will eventually determine his or her destiny.

- Be consistent.

- Be a good example.

- Follow through.

# 3

# STRUCTURE

*"Rules are important, but example is the great stimulus."*

ZIG ZIGLAR

*AUTHOR AND
MOTIVATIONAL EXPERT*

Structure is the blueprint of a child's character. Without it, we wouldn't have a foundation for character building. Structure holds the pillars of a success in place. Imagine driving to work or the mall with no lines on the road, no street signs, and no laws to follow. What would you have? Chaos! That is why boundaries and guidelines are so important in a child's life. Before you can teach kids respect, discipline, self control, perseverance, focus, and integrity, you have to establish your expectations of them. If you want your kids to do their homework when they get home from school – make it a rule and enforce it. If you want them in bed by 8:00, make them go to bed at 8:00 and not a minute later. If you want them to eat the right foods, select a menu and stick to it. I could go on and I will, but not now. The younger they are, the more structure they need and the more rigid you have to be. You can lighten up as they get older and they prove to be more responsible. But be careful not to lighten up too much, too soon. Some children mature faster than others. They will seem to act and talk like an adult. They want to be treated like a grown up. Some children seem so mature that we forget they're still ten years old. No matter how mature kids seem, don't forget that they're still children and they still need your structure and your guidance. Remember, they may be intellectually or physically mature for their age but their emotional maturity is still that of a child.

Without structure, my martial arts business wouldn't work. When students come into my school, they know where they should wait for class. They know where to put their shoes and they know when their class begins. We even have spots on the floor that show students where to stand throughout the class. If they stray from those spots without permission, they could receive a kick accidentally or kick someone else. I also recommend to parents that they adhere to a structured class schedule. They should attend class consistently on Tuesdays and Thursdays for example. This way the child knows that after school on those days his or her schedule includes the martial arts class. He knows when to expect homework time, snack time, play time, martial arts time, and bedtime. He has structure. Scheduling helps kids compartmentalize and avoid mixing their activities, such as homework and play time.

## SHOW ME A KID WHO'S IN TOO MANY EXTRACURRICULAR ACTIVITIES, AND I'LL SHOW YOU A MISERABLE PARENT

Beware: Don't commit your kids to too many structured activities. As with everything else in life, they need to maintain a balance. Don't give your kid too much structured time. Being part of sports teams can be very valuable because kids learn a lot about teamwork and structure, but having too many sports commitments will have an adverse affect. Many parents at my school struggle with bringing their kids to class because they have too many other sports or lessons. If you've ever said the following, or something like it, we need to talk. "I'm just having a hard time getting him here because he has baseball practice three days a week and a game on Saturday. He has gymnastics on Tuesdays and piano on Thursdays. On top of that, his sister has dance at the same time as his piano, and her ice skating lessons are after his baseball practice on Mondays. Somewhere in there, they have to do their homework. I'm having a hard time juggling this schedule and being the mommy chauffeur." Are you kidding me people? Having kids is supposed to be fun and enjoyable! Nobody is happy with this situation. Mom is miserable and the kids are miserable. Mom has no time for herself, and junior has no time to relax and play.

I recommend having one sport and one personal development activity, such as piano or tutoring, at a time. I strongly suggest martial arts as a personal development activity because it combines the benefits of fitness *and* character development. Martial arts actually complements and improves other sports and activities too. Please don't over-do it with activities and commitments. Let your kid be a kid. They'll have plenty of time to be overworked when they grow up. Find a balance and stick to it.

## Points to Remember

- Establish structure. Without structure, you have chaos.
- The younger the child, the more rigid the structure.
- Avoid committing your child to too many structured activities.
- Be consistent.
- Be a good example.
- Follow through.

# CONDITIONING

*"Parents are handing life's scripts to their children, scripts that in all likelihood will be acted out for much of the rest of the children's lives."*

STEPHEN R. COVEY

*AUTHOR OF SEVEN HABITS OF HIGHLY EFFECTIVE PEOPLE*

The behaviorist Ivan Pavlov conditioned his dogs to salivate every time he rang a bell. He did this by ringing a bell and then feeding his dogs immediately. After much repetition, the dogs understood that the bell meant food. Pavlov eventually evoked salivation just by ringing the bell. His dogs had learned an association between hearing the bell and satisfying their hunger. This conditioning occurred thanks to reinforcement and repetition. Conditioning teaches your child to follow a certain structure. This is a critical part of parenting and Character Coaching. Kids can and should be conditioned - not in a laboratory type setting but in a loving parental setting. When our son Aidan was a baby, we stuck to a schedule. We fed him at approximately the same times daily and we had specified play time. We put him to bed the same time every night. Because we stuck to a basic schedule, we conditioned him. There was very little guess work about when he would be hungry. We rarely wondered when he would take a nap which freed us to make appointments or run scheduled errands. There was very little question about when he would go to bed at night so my wife and I could count on alone time. By sticking with this structure, we had more freedom and the joy of a well behaved, predictable little boy. I have friends whose kids run their lives because they don't impose structure. They're unable to go out to eat at a restaurant with us. They can't make plans because they don't know when their kids are going to be hungry. They certainly can't hire a babysitter and see a movie alone because they don't know when the baby is going to bed. They don't get much sleep and they're not happy people. How do they live like this? This lifestyle's not for me. Is it for you? Conditioning a child to accept structure makes Mom, Dad, and the child so much happier. Some may say that my wife and I just lucked out - that Aidan is just a good-natured boy. Is it luck? Is it structure? Is it both? The one thing I know for sure is if you have no structure, your child will be completely unpredictable, and that will wear you out.

## DON'T HEAR WHAT I'M NOT SAYING

I'm not saying that parenting is a lab experiment. I know that talk about conditioning sounds a little cold, but it's really not. It's a necessary part of raising kids. Remember, you are your child's teacher. You are teaching your child how to live. And we all want our kids to have a great life. Being a loving parent is always the most important part of being Mom or Dad. I love my son and he knows it. He also knows that I am guiding him to success. If you still don't like the word "conditioning," think of it as becoming accustomed to certain behaviors and expectations. You and your child both become accustomed to certain things. I can't tell you how many times I've had plans to run an errand on my way to work and arrived in my normal parking spot without running the errand. My brain just goes on autopilot and I keep driving my normal route to work instead of making the left turn to go to the bank. This is conditioning. We want to set our child up with an autopilot. Brian Tracy in his *Million Dollar Habits* says, "Beginning in childhood, you develop a series of conditioned responses that lead you to react automatically and unthinkingly in almost every situation." It is possible to set your child's autopilot to take them in good directions.

As a teacher of life, approach your lessons from different levels. You must guide children with love and you must teach them from a cognitive level. You know more about this world than your child, and you need to develop ways to share your knowledge with your child.

There is an art and a science to parenting and that is the focus of this book. Follow the principles in these pages, and you will enjoy your kids more than ever, and they, in turn, will get much more out of life.

**Points to Remember**

- Conditioning is programming your child to follow a certain structure.

- Establish structure in their lives, along with a set of rules to govern them.

- Help them become accustomed to certain expectations so they become automatic.

- Make sure your child's autopilot takes them in good directions.

- Condition them for success.

- Be consistent.

- Be a good example.

- Follow through.

# 5

# DISCIPLINE

*"Let thy child's first lesson be obedience, and the
second will be what thou wilt."*

**BENJAMIN FRANKLIN**
*INVENTOR AND STATESMAN*

It's vital for parents and teachers to lay down rules and inspire kids to follow them. The sooner you teach children about boundaries and the consequences of misbehavior, the better. In other words, discipline your children. Discipline means training your kids to follow structure. As Dr. Terry Alderman, national educational consultant and developer of *Discipline: A Total Approach*, says "discipline is love. Discipline is something we do for a child, not to a child."

Many parents bring their children to me for the discipline. Martial Arts has always had a reputation for instilling discipline in young people. It goes with the territory. Imagine if I had a room full of kids who all knew how to kick and punch but had no discipline. Worse yet, imagine how these same, undisciplined kids with these skills might interact with friends and family members outside the martial arts school. Discipline is for their safety and for respect of others. That's what it boils down to. Many parents forget that the main purpose of disciplining their children is for their safety and happiness. Too often, parents don't discipline their children because it seems mean, or they're afraid it will affect their relationship negatively. Sometimes, parents fail to discipline because they just don't know how. If more parents would just remember why they should discipline their children, they would have an easier time actually doing it.

## KIDS LOVE DISCIPLINE AND DISCIPLINE IS LOVE

Kids don't just need discipline; they want it. It's so fundamental, they almost beg for it. Discipline is like the railings on a narrow rope bridge. They keep you going in a straight line so you won't deviate laterally. It's more fun and less nerve-racking to cross these bridges knowing that the railings are there if you need them. You can try to go for it on your own, but you want the security of knowing those rails are there. Kids feel more secure if they understand their boundaries. When children decide to play a game of football or soccer in the yard, first they pick teams and then they decide what's out of bounds. If kids don't have boundaries and rules, they make up their own which can be a disastrous proposition! Kids without discipline are like runaway cars without drivers. They may be free to go anywhere they want, but with nothing to direct them, they're a danger to themselves and everyone and everything around.

I explain to my new students very early that if they can't follow the rules and do as I tell them, I am not willing to teach them. I show them where their shoes belong and why. I tell them that they must be barefoot on the workout floor. I talk about how we wear our uniforms and belts to every class. I let them know how important it is to be punctual. I clearly explain my expectations of them and I then hold them to it. If later, I find their shoes out of place, I will pull the student out of class and ask the child to put them where they belong. If they use their skills inappropriately, or have bad conduct at school, they will not receive their next belt. If a child is not following the rules of the martial arts school, there are serious consequences.

Parents and teachers have the responsibility of teaching children that there are consequences for everything. If the child does something well, they should be rewarded for it proportionately. At the same time, if she breaks the rules, she should experience the negative, proportionate consequence. I tell my students that if they behave inappropriately at martial arts class, school, or home, they will not be promoted to their next belt level. I have to remain firm on this, or the kids will catch on quickly that I am just talking the talk and not walking it. Kids are clever. If they do not experience some sort of punishment for wrong behavior, they will never adjust that behavior. They know when they can get away with actions and when they can't. Parents and teachers alike have to inform kids of the consequences of unacceptable behaviors and then follow through consistently.

## FOLLOW THROUGH

Consistent follow through is one of the biggest challenges parents or teachers face when disciplining children. We have all known someone who was all talk. We knew that if we broke their rule, they would probably just express their disappointment verbally but not follow through with actual consequences. When I first started teaching children martial arts, I would promise students a punishment for an unacceptable behavior, but when they actually did it, I didn't have the nerve to follow through. I was too worried that they would hate me for disciplining them or that they would quit taking lessons. I remember a particular instance where one of my students was receiving poor conduct grades in school. I told her that if she didn't improve in that area, I wouldn't promote her to her next belt. When her next progress report came around, she had not improved. Instead of sticking to the consequences, I gave her the ole, "I'll give it to you this time, but next time I want you to bring up that conduct grade," and I promoted her anyway. I couldn't help it. She was so sweet to me and her big innocent eyes made me give in. Sound familiar? So, who's the sucker? That's right - me. Did she learn anything from this? Yes - she learned that I don't follow through and she doesn't have to fulfill my expectations, because I don't have the guts to punish her.

I have since learned that kids don't quit martial arts if I follow through with the consequences, and they actually respect me more and try harder. Kids will only respect and follow direction from someone who has a backbone. Remember, the more often you give in to kids, the less they look up to you and want to please you. Kids know when your warnings are followed up with just more warnings. The more you "punish" with warnings, the more they are going to act up. Almost as bad as empty threats, is just tolerating their behavior. As Dr. Alderman says, "If you tolerate it, you tend to teach it." Putting up with a behavior over and over not only sends them a message that they can get away with anything; it will also drive you mad.

## THE BUDDY APPROACH

One of the biggest mistakes parents make when raising their kids is that they try to take the buddy approach. The problem is that kids don't take orders from a buddy. Don't be afraid to show your kid who's boss. If you don't establish the hierarchy as early as possible, you can plan on your kids running your life. No adults fare well when kids dictate their lives. In my line of work, I have seen so many parents bring their kids to me and ask me to help their child with some "small behavior issues." After watching the parent and child interact, I know exactly what is going on. They could have just said to me, "Please discipline my kids because I am by no stretch of the imagination an authority figure. I'm just a kid too." These parents are trying to be too cool. They are trying to be their child's friend. I know it's tempting to be "cool and fun" to your kids all of the time, but at some point someone has to be the adult. Kids need parents, not friends.

When I began teaching children martial arts, I wanted to be the coolest instructor in the school. I wanted to be fun, and I wanted everyone to like me. Because I didn't know any better, I tried to be everyone's friend. For a while (a very short while), it worked. They eventually began to take advantage of me and learned to not take me seriously as an authority figure. I soon lost control. I had to work long and hard to regain their respect as a professional. I learned to be friendly, without being their friend.

## PRAISE, CORRECT, PRAISE

When it comes to correcting or criticizing kids, you have to do it delicately to remain effective. At my school, we use P.C.P., which stands for Praise, Correct, Praise. If a child is not performing in a way that is expected, we avoid the temptation to yell at them. Saying something like, "Hey stupid, you're not doing that right," will certainly cause an effect – it will worsen the behavior. It's best to handle corrections in a way that fits that child's personality. You must be firm, but positive. Correcting a child's actions can be a great learning opportunity that also raises their self esteem.

The next time one of your kids is not behaving properly, try this approach. First, be a good-finder. Find something that they're doing right and praise them for it. Then ask if you can show them how to do it better. Next, make the appropriate correction. Wait for them to make the change and when they do, praise them again. For example, if I see a child doing his side kick wrong because he's not bending his knee enough, here's how I would approach it: "Stephen, you're doing that side kick so high. I can't believe how high you can raise your leg! You must be doing your stretches at home. Can I show you how to make your side kick more powerful?" When you ask their permission to help them, kids feel like they're in control. Children thrive on respect shown by adults. By "allowing" you to help them, they subconsciously become more open to learning. So use that opening to instruct them further. "If you will just bend your knee and pull it back a little farther, you'll be able to kick with much more force." I usually demonstrate the kick myself and then pull the child's leg back for him. This way I know I'm clear since I am using a proven method to teach children.

Kids differ from one another in the process in which they learn. The three processes are: auditory (listening), visual (seeing), and kinesthetic (touching or moving). I try to address the three learning processes every time I can, since I can't always remember every child's individual needs. For example, I told Stephen the steps to take to improve. Then I showed him how to do it. And finally, I allowed him to feel the correction by moving his leg for him. After I make the correction, I follow up with: "Can you try that for me?" After making the change, I praise him by telling him how awesome he is and remark on the great improvement he has made. I'll then tell him that he's going to make a great Black Belt some day and I finish off with a high five. With these actions, I accomplished three things. I improved Stephen's side kick, raised his self esteem, and developed more trust and respect between us.

By using P.C.P., you can change your child's performance or behavior and raise his or her self esteem. If I had just said to Stephen: "Bend your knee more," the results would have been much different. It's quite possible that he wouldn't have fully understood what I meant. Most likely he would have continued doing it the old way making more corrections necessary. If we continued with this pattern, Stephen's kick would never improve and he'd begin to doubt whether he was good at martial arts. Use P.C.P. all of the time no matter the subject matter. Your kids are bound to improve and become more confident in the process.

## PUNISHMENT

Discipline is the structure you provide for a child while punishment is the action you take when the discipline is not working. Punishment is a necessary evil and is the consequence of bad behavior. It's negative reinforcement that will deter a child from repeating an action. Touching a hot pan is painful and provides memorable negative reinforcement. The pain will most likely make enough of an impression to keep the child from doing it again.

Every human being instinctively avoids pain and pursues pleasure. That's why punishment works. If you punish a child by taking away something they value like freedom to go to a friend's house or the TV, later they will avoid that pain and move towards behaviors that will grant them more pleasure.

The punishment must fit the crime. Use good judgment when punishing your child. If they've committed a small offense, the punishment should be small. The larger the offense, the more extreme the punishment. When I was young, my mother and father had different levels of punishment depending on the offense. Punishments ranged from a simple reprimand to a good old fashion spanking. I hated the spankings, but when I look back now, I can honestly admit that I never received one I didn't deserve and they were very effective.

I will not explore the controversy of physical punishment. That topic is beyond the scope of this book. I will say that if a particular form of punishment does not send the necessary message to your child, then it needs to be more severe. Note to teachers and other professional Character Coaches: Obviously, physical punishment is not an option for you. However, there are different levels of punishment that are acceptable in your situation, such as withholding privileges, sending a note home, or even worse, making them go to the principal's office.

In all fairness, kids do deserve a warning before punishment. They don't always know or remember when they've broken a rule. They need a yellow light to let them know that if they continue on their current course, they will be punished. The yellow light can be a verbal warning or even a hand signal. In a class setting, I use different types of warnings. First, I use proximity if the bad behavior is still in an early stage. I simply stand next to them while I'm teaching. If a child is acting up considerably, I tell them quietly that they can do better, and if they don't, they will be punished.

I never yell across the room at a child since this only results in embarrassment, more bad behavior and a blow to their self esteem. I even have a physical cue that I use when warning kids from a long distance. It can be as simple as pointing a finger at them with a stern face. These are nip-it-in-the-bud warnings. If the behavior continues, it's time to deliver the appropriate punishment. Remember, if these warnings go unheeded, you must follow up with consequences. Don't give empty threats. Always follow through. Again, I always punish privately. Punishment is designed to put the child back on track, not to demoralize them. Don't yell at them in front of friends or classmates.

Since we shouldn't punish publicly, here are a couple of ways you relay a message to a group of children without singling someone out. These methods can work whether you're a coach on the field, a teacher in the classroom, or a parent at a birthday party. If a child is talking while I'm talking and a few gentle reminders don't stop his behavior, I bring all the kids together and huddle up. I get down on my knees so I'm communicating to them at their eye level. Then, I ask the whole group what can happen if someone is talking out of turn while I'm talking. The kids will usually give me great answers on their own. Then I ask the group if they can all do a better job listening when I'm talking. Usually the challenging child will conform. Another way to get the point across to a challenging child is by spotlighting a child who is behaving appropriately. For example, you can say to the whole class, "Look how Martha is sitting still with her back straight, her hands on her knees, and her eyes and ears are focused on me. Can everyone do this?" Often, this does the trick.

Rewarding good behavior is often an effective way to motivate challenging children to improve their behavior. For some kids, punishment will not steer them toward better behavior. They don't mind getting in trouble because at least then, they are getting some attention. We need a different plan of action for them. These kids will often respond to praise and rewards. If a troublesome kid sees other children getting rewards such as privileges, treats, or more freedom, they will also pursue better behavior. Be sure to publicly praise children who are being a good example so others will follow in their footsteps.

Remember, kids don't want to be bad. Be sure they know the appropriate behaviors you expect as well as the consequences for bad behavior and the rewards for good behavior. Give them one warning, not 3 or 4, and then follow through.

## Points to Remember

- Establish rules, consequences and rewards. Remind them that rules are for their safety.

- Enforce those rules.

- Follow through with consequences and rewards.

- Kids need parents, not adult buddies.

- Praise them when you are correcting them.

- Use punishment to get them back on track when their behavior is unacceptable.

- Punish kids privately, not publicly.

- Follow through with consequences or rules will become meaningless.

- Be consistent.

- Be a good example.

- Follow through.

# 6

# INFLUENCE

*"You are the average of the five people you*
*spend the most time with."*

**JIM ROHN**

*BEST SELLING AUTHOR*
*AND MOTIVATIONAL SPEAKER*

It is inevitable that the world around kids and the people in it are going to influence them. The world is full of negative and positive influences. It is important, now more than ever, that we screen our kids' influences and act as a positive role model. Children (and adults for that matter) are very impressionable. The people and behaviors that they're exposed to will fashion their character. As Character Coaches, we have to outweigh the negative influences by being a positive mentor and exposing them to good role models, friends, and programs.

What do you do on a consistent and constant basis to ensure your child's success? I can tell you what the rest of the world is doing on a constant and consistent basis.

Advertisers are constantly bombarding your kids with ads that influence them to be someone they aren't and someone we don't want them to be. Programs on TV are becoming more and more violent and sexual. Even some of the "children's programs" are full of characters who are conniving and smart-alecky. The most popular music hits are full of profanity and overt sexuality.

What about school? Unfortunately, school can be a source of negativity and bad influence. We already know the negative effect that bullying and peer pressure have on your child, but what about

37

the more subtle influences? I can tell you that your kid is exposed to the following statements everyday. "More me, less you." "It's all fun until you get caught." "I love my attitude problem." "It's all about me." "90% devil, 10% angel." "I used to think I was lazy, so I stopped thinking." "I live in time-out." And there are more, lots more. These phrases are on T-shirts everywhere. Kids as young as kindergarten wear them. Come on, people! The scary thing is that they are very popular. I teach my success principles and martial arts at local public schools and when I'm there, I make note of the T-shirts the kids are wearing. I don't know which disturbs me more - the fact that the kids are wearing these statements, the fact that their parents bought these shirts for them, or the fact that someone actually manufactures them. By buying them and letting their kid wear them, parents endorse that behavior. I wonder how these parents would react if their child actually lived by these statements. If parents let them live this way, the parents should be put away. If they don't, then they are hypocrites. Buying these T-shirts but expecting good behavior is sending a mixed message to the kids. I know wearing certain T-shirts doesn't sound like a big deal, but constant exposure to anything, big or small, even at a subliminal level, will eventually leak into your child's character. All of this negativity isn't going away any time soon. It's our responsibility as Character Coaches to arm our children against these influences.

### BIRDS OF A FEATHER FLOCK TOGETHER.

On top of messages from the advertising and the entertainment industries, we have to worry about the company our kids keep. Remember, attitudes are contagious. If we allow our kids to hang out with certain crowds, they become part of that crowd. Dr. David McClelland of Harvard calls these crowds their "reference group." He says that this group can determine 95% of your success or failure in life. In his book *Success- One Day At a Time,* John C. Maxwell says "if you place a hot poker near the heat of a fire, it too becomes hot. To succeed (or fail), follow the hot poker principle." Mr. Maxwell also provides us with the following story that helps illustrate to your child the importance of the company we keep.

*For years, Monterey, California, was a pelican's paradise. The town was the site of many fish canneries. In fact, it was the home of Cannery*

*Row, a street popularized by Nobel Prize-winning author John Steinbeck in his novel of that name. Pelicans loved the town because fisherman cleaned their catch, discarding the offal, and the pelicans would feast on those scraps. In Monterey, any pelican could be well fed without having to work for a meal.*

*But as time went by, the fish along the California coast were depleted, and one by one, the canneries all shut down. That's when the pelicans got into trouble. You see, pelicans are naturally great fishers. They fly in groups over the waves of the sea, and when they find fish, they dive into the water and scoop up their catch. But these pelicans hadn't fished in years. They had grown fat and lazy. And now that their easy meals were gone, they were actually starving.*

*Environmentalists from the area wracked their brains to figure out a way to help the pelicans, and finally they came up with a solution. They imported pelicans from another area, ones that were used to foraging every day, and they mixed them in with the local birds. The newcomers immediately started fishing for their own food, and it wasn't long before the starving native birds joined them and started fishing for themselves again.*[1]

When talking to your kids about the company they keep, tell them this story, and ask them the following questions.

### FOLLOW-UP QUESTIONS

1. How did the native birds re-learn how to fish?
2. Do you see how we become like the people we are around the most?
3. What kind of people should we hang out with?
   a. Kids who are always getting in trouble at school?
   b. Kids who do drugs or smoke cigarettes?
   c. Kids who use bad or negative language?
   d. Nice kids who are fun and always follow the rules?

### MESSAGE

It is important that we stay away from negative people. They are more dangerous than bullies and monsters. They are putting garbage into our minds that will have a long-term negative effect. Always seek friendship with kids who follow rules and have a good attitude.

## WHAT ARE WE GOING TO DO ABOUT IT?

So far, anyone reading this book (who doesn't know me) might think I'm a very negative person. They might think that my answer to good parenting is sheltering our kids. This is not me at all! I am very positive and I certainly don't think sheltering your child is an answer. In fact, I think kids should be subjected to a less-than-perfect environment. They should go through trials and tribulations. They should be exposed to *some* negative things. They should get their feelings hurt. They should scrape their knees while playing. They should lose a pet or a best friend to a move. They should have peers pressure them. This is all part of growing up. Without these experiences, they will not grow up with strong enough backbones to become real successes. There is no escaping bad stuff. It gets worse the older you get. Avoiding it is never the answer. Facing it and dealing with it is.

By now, you must be confused. Am I being hypocritical here? No. No matter how good a Character Coach you are or become, there will always be negativity in the world. It is our job to limit their exposure to the bad stuff as much as we can and advocate the good stuff more. It's important that we raise our kids with enough character so when they're exposed to the bad stuff, the experience will only strengthen them, not weaken them. With a strong character, your child will not only succeed in a negative world, he or she will have the power to change the world. It's up to you, Mom. It's up to you, Dad. It's up to you, Character Coach. You must prepare your kids. You have to train them to be successful. Your influence and teaching must be more consistent, constant, effective, loving and powerful than anything the world can throw at them. Your teachings must become habits. In the following chapters I will give you and your child even more tools they will need to be successful.

## YOU'RE NOT ALONE.

There are many great role models out there to help you. Not only are they helpful, they're a necessity. Just like you and other Character Coaches, I need other influences for my children. I know that my son will only listen to me so much. He will need to hear the same values and ethics I teach him from someone else. I see this all of the time as a professional Character Coach. My clients are always telling me that they tried to make something clear to their kid, but it didn't work. They couldn't get through to them. As their martial arts instructor, if I tell them the exact same thing their parents told them, it has a much more profound effect. You can find positive role models for your kids in so many settings. Take the time to see if their sports coaches are good influences. Check to see how effective their academic teachers are as role models. Investigate their paid extracurricular activities like gymnastics, music and martial arts. Use friends' referrals. It doesn't take much time and energy to find good people who can be a positive influence for your child.

Use these role models to the best of your advantage. My clients use me like a year-round Santa Claus. "If you don't clean up your room right now young man, I am going to tell Mr. Klapheke!" I hear examples like this all the time. I don't mind that parents use me as a threat. In fact, I encourage it. Whatever motivates them to perform is good for me. The point is, you can take some of the heat off yourself if you have another role model in your child's life.

## POINTS TO REMEMBER

- Children are constantly bombarded by outside influences - usually not good ones.
- Your influence should have more power than any other.
- Kids become like the kids they hang out with. Screen their friends, teachers, friends' parents and coaches.
- Employ professional role models to help out.
- Be consistent.
- Be a good example.
- Follow through.

# PART II

## THE
## PILLARS OF
## GOOD
## CHARACTER

# 7

# RESPECT

*"Do unto others as you would have them do unto you."*

**JESUS OF NAZARETH**

Everyone in the world wants to feel respected. It is one of the most important feelings of validation a person can have. One major reason people want to be rich and famous is because they know that people will treat them differently. The truth is it doesn't take fame and fortune to garner respect. You gain respect by showing other people respect *and* respecting yourself. Teaching children how to respect themselves and others will improve their quality of life significantly. I believe it's a parent's responsibility to teach their children about respect, including the true meaning of respect.

The first step is to make sure that you, as a Character Coach, respect yourself enough to be your child's role model. In all my life, I've never had a great desire for a friend or sibling to tell me what to do or to boss me around. However, I have appreciated their opinions - as long as they were similar to mine. The only people I've allowed to actually lead me were the people who I wanted to be like or who intimidated me.

People who are intimidating have a strong presence. They demand respect, and they get it. They want to be treated like they are important and consequently, they are. Character Coaches should emulate people who demand respect. We can't be perceived as push-overs or people who appear to be weak. True Character Coaches impress others and naturally lead them. Everyone has role models like this in their lives - people that you want to please, people whose approval is high on your priority list. You avoid getting into trouble with them not just because you fear the punishment, but because you don't want to disappoint them. Parents in particular should always strive to be people who command this kind of respect.

Whether you are a parent, martial arts instructor or a teacher, your kids need you to be their role model, not their friend. Kids have plenty of peers who can be their friends. I've seen many parents who try so hard to be "cool" with their kids or avoid punishing them out of fear that their kids won't like them anymore. Their children are always the most difficult kids to have in my classes. These kids don't respect their parents and haven't been taught how to respect other people. They talk back, don't share, don't listen and don't cooperate. In the end, they don't learn much in class and they rarely make friends.

There is a direct correlation between their behavior towards others and their relationship with their parents. How is a child going to respect himself, much less anyone else, if his own parents don't respect themselves enough to guide their children with authority? That's why it is so important to be a parent, not a buddy. Kids won't respect you if you bring yourself down to their level. Being a buddy actually shows a lack of leadership and self esteem. Being a good parent is tough to do sometimes but you have to be the alpha in order to foster respect from your child.

## PROTOCOL

Teaching your children protocol is the next step to becoming an effective Character Coach. Demand that they answer your questions with a "yes, sir" or a "yes, ma'am." Then make it very clear that they are not to argue with you. There will be no talking back, disobedience, or breaking the rules. Spell out your expectations and the consequences of misbehavior. Do it with confidence, assertiveness and consistency.

When a kid comes into my school for the first time, I teach them about respect before anything else. It's the foundation for my class. First, I introduce myself to him and look him in the eye while I wait for his response. If he doesn't look me in the eye, I will politely ask him to look at me and tell me his name. I make it a point to let him know that I am important and that he is important too. Many times during the first lesson, I have to remind the new student that he should always maintain eye contact. If the child isn't looking at me while I'm talking to him or while he's talking to me, I remind him that we're in class to learn from our instructors and not to look around the room. I don't want him to think that the punching bag or poster is more important than my instructions.

Next, I explain to the new student the meaning of respect. To put it simply, respect means being nice to people. It means treating them like they're important because they are. I teach students to treat others the way they want others to treat them. I explain that it is important to show respect in class because only then will I teach them karate.

Parents should explain the consequences of disrespect from their kids, such as not allowing kids to go to a friend's house or banning their video games or other activities they enjoy. I also explain that if they call people names, make fun of or pick fights, they are being disrespectful and this is no way for a martial artist to behave. If they can't be respectful of others, then I can't trust them with their new skills outside of the karate school. Similarly as a parent, you can explain that you can't trust them to go over to a friend's house or go to a birthday party if they can't show respect for others.

After discussing the importance of respect, I always tell my students to show me that they understand by saying "yes, sir." I reiterate that replying with "sirs" and "ma'ams" lets older people or people of authority know that kids are listening and understand the importance of their words. I tell them that this applies to their mom and dad, coaches, teachers, or any adult. Then I ask the student: "Can you do that for me?" If he answers with a "yeah", or an "uh huh", or even a "yes," I bust him. "What does "yeah" mean?" I ask him. "I don't know what that word is." Then almost without fail, he says, "Yes, sir." Throughout the whole first lesson I reinforce that behavior several times until it becomes a habit. After several lessons, the children say "yes, sir" because they are truly learning to respect others.

Once your kids understand the meaning of respect and how to show it, you must stay on them to really make it stick. All principles of good character are transformed into habits with constant reinforcement. Let kids know how proud you are when they show respect. Then show them respect in return. Let them know how good it feels. You can show your child respect in a number of ways. For example, don't interrupt your child. What he is saying is very important to him. Look at him and give him your full attention when he is talking. Say "yes, sir" to him. Treat him the way you want him to treat you, with the understanding that you are the authority figure.

## TEACHING FROM A PEDESTAL

Remember, never let kids think they are your equal. I see this happen all of the time at karate schools, even at my own. I am in a business where I work with kids for several consecutive years unlike teachers at school. After a long period of time I naturally develop such a rapport with them, they're almost like family. If I'm not careful, they will slowly lower the pedestal that they placed me on when they first joined the school. These kids develop a comfort level with me, and if I don't keep them in check, they start to act less and less like a student, and more like an equal. I have to remain on an unreachable level to them or I won't have anything to offer them.

If they think that I'm their buddy, they try to get away with more. The longer a student is with me, the *friendlier* I become with them, but I do not become their *friend*. I also have to resist the urge of acting too silly or childlike around them because I'd be at their level again. I'm not suggesting that you have to take yourself too seriously to teach children. Anyone who knows me knows this is not the case. The point of keeping yourself on a higher level is to give them someone to look up to. If you don't have the confidence to feel that you are "pedestal worthy," then I suggest that you fake it. There's an old adage that says, "Fake it 'til you make it." If you have to pretend you are confident enough to lead a child, then do it. If you do a good job of faking it, believe it or not, you'll eventually convince your kids **and** yourself.

I am not advocating that you become a stick in the mud and have no fun. I'm all about fun. You should absolutely play with your kids and it's okay to be a kid yourself for a little while. Just be sure to change gears again afterward. We all want to be kids again on occasion, and we should take advantage of having kids to do that. Just watch out. After you play together, kids need a transition back to protocol. It's a fact that kids are known to try to get away with something immediately following goof off time. They may even ask you for something you've resisted in the past. Kids are smart. Watch out.

## KEEPING THEM IN CHECK

The majority of kids will slip up every once in a while and forget to respect their authority figures. They don't mean to be disrespectful; they just forget to show respect sometimes, especially with their parents. These are the times when we should gently remind them of our expectations. Sometimes, I can do this with my students by just giving them a look of dissatisfaction. It takes me time to get to that level with some kids, but it is possible. Sometimes I have to tell them that they're not showing adequate respect. As a reminder, I tell the story of the Black Belt Who Didn't Bow. You can tell the same story to your kids even if they aren't martial arts students because the point of the story is a good one. After telling the story, use the follow-up questions and the message that follows.

*A boy named Noah who had been training in the martial arts for over three years, received his Black Belt from Master Chin. Soon after his promotion, Master Chin noticed that Noah wasn't following the proper protocol of the school. The boy didn't say "yes, sir" or "no, sir;" and started coming to class late. What's more, he didn't perform with as much enthusiasm as he had before. He even quit bowing to Master Chin at the start of the classes.*

*Master Chin was very concerned and asked Noah to stay after class and have a talk with him. When he asked Noah why he was behaving this way, Noah said, "Well, now that I'm a Black Belt, I thought that it wasn't as important to act the way I did before. After all, you know that I respect you so I didn't think I had to show you all of the time now that I'm a Black Belt, too." Master Chin said nothing.*

*Something very unexpected happened the next time Noah came to class. Master Chin walked up to Noah and took his Black Belt from him and replaced it with a white belt. With a look of disbelief, Noah asked him why he did that. Master Chin responded, "Everyone knows that you're a Black Belt so I figured we don't need to show everybody all of the time." Noah learned his lesson very quickly - it's not enough to have respect for people, you also have to show it often, even if you feel like an equal.*

## FOLLOW-UP QUESTIONS

1. Should we just assume that someone knows that we respect or love them?

2. How can you show people you care about that you respect them?

3. Is it okay to stop showing respect to your teachers or parents just because you've known them for a long time?

## MESSAGE

It's not enough to just know in your heart that you respect someone; you have to show it on a regular basis, even with the little things like saying "sir" and "ma'am."

My students call me Mr. Klapheke. After being students for a long time, a few inevitably ask me if they can start calling me "Daniel." That's a big N-O. I ask them: "What has changed? Do you feel like I'm a different person to you now that you're older? Don't forget, I'm older too and I am still your instructor." I've had a couple of students ask if they need to call me Mr. Klapheke outside the karate school. I answer with a similar line of questioning. "Why would our relationship be different at another location? Do you call your mom "Betty" when you are at the grocery store and call her "Mom" when you're at home?" Usually the point becomes clear to them then. The bottom line is to make sure that kids understand that they can't turn respect on and off like a switch.

## THE GOLDEN RULE

It's important for kids to understand that they should show respect to everyone, not just their elders. Respect is about treating everybody with consideration – doing unto others the way they want others to do unto them. Remind them of the Golden Rule with this story:

*One day a little boy who was really mad at his mother ran out of the house to the hillside and shouted into the valley, "I hate you." Back from the valley came the echo, "I hate you!" Confused and hurt, he ran back into the house and told his mother there was someone in the valley yelling they hated him.*

*His mother took him back to the hillside and told him to yell, "I love you!" He did as his mother said, and this time he discovered there was someone in the valley saying, "I love you."*[2]

## FOLLOW-UP QUESTIONS

1. If you are nice to other people, will they be mean or nice to you in return?

2. How would someone be treated if he/she treated everyone with meanness?

3. Would you like someone who was rude to you and treated you poorly?

## MESSAGE

Life is like an echo. The message you send out—comes back. The actions you sow—you reap. The treatment you give—you get. The characteristics you see in others—exist in you. Regardless of who you are or what you do, if you're looking for the best way to reap the most reward in all areas of life, you should look for the good in every person and in every situation.

The better your child understands respect and how to show it, the more rewarding his life will be. Be consistent and constantly remind your child about the importance of respect. Establishing this habit at home will certainly carry over to all areas of his life.

## MANNERS AND COURTESY

Who doesn't like a kid with good manners? Regardless of his looks, intelligence or background, if a kid is polite and courteous, people will respond to him. Imagine you are a teacher and one of your students is on the honor roll with perfect attendance. However, this student is unfortunately very rude and doesn't show respect for anyone else's feelings. Another of your students has below average grades and is frightfully forgetful. This student fortunately has great manners which he shows by saying "please" and "thank you" or "yes, sir" or "yes, ma'am." He holds the door for you and always volunteers to help. Which kid will you naturally want to help when they need it? People are drawn to good people. They enjoy the sweet kid while they merely tolerate the brat.

Teach your children to say "please" and "thank you," to answer with a "yes, sir' or 'yes, ma'am," and to hold the door for others. Make sure they introduce themselves, shake hands and maintain eye contact, and listen without interrupting or ignoring. Teach them to be punctual and value other people's time, not talk with a full mouth, to cover when they cough or sneeze, to say excuse me and to help people who need help. A person who lacks these qualities will surely lack respect in life while a person who demonstrates care and concern will earn respect all along the way.

## POINTS TO REMEMBER

- Your children will not respect you if you are not a loving alpha.
- First, you must respect yourself.
- Don't be a push over.
- Don't try to be their friend. They have plenty of those. Be their parent.
- Teach them the meaning of respect and how to show it. Then demand it.
- Tell them the stories I've provided and ask follow-up questions.
- Be consistent.
- Be a good example.
- Follow through.

# 8

# SELF CONTROL

*"Most powerful is he who has himself in his own power."*

LUCIUS ANNAEUS SENECA
*ROMAN PHILOSOPHER*

Self control, as defined by the Oxford Dictionary of Current English, is the power to control one's behavior and emotions. The next lesson that I teach new students is how to control themselves. I make it very clear that Martial Arts is only for self defense and should never be used to harm someone, unless it is an emergency. I explain to the new students that I can only teach them skills when I trust them to control themselves. I don't want them to be tempted to use their newfound skills to be a bully, show off, or intimidate their friends or family. I make them prove their power of self control by teaching them an attention stance. Students are not allowed to move while in this position. All they can do is blink their eyes and breathe. There's no scratching, no looking around, and certainly no talking while I'm talking. I make them do this for several seconds at a time for as many as 10 reps in a row, until they understand my expectations.

## PHYSICAL CONTROL

Next, I explain the importance of physical control and how we will use it in later lessons doing more difficult techniques. If students can't control their bodies while standing in one place, they'll have a tough time later when I ask them to jump, spin, kick and land on their feet again. I make my point about physical control with a "cool" example – how a Black Belt behaves. Then I challenge them to do the same in the classroom. I ask them, "Do you think a Black Belt would ever show off their karate skills in school?" "No Sir!" they reply. "Do you think a Black Belt would sit still in his desk at school or would he look around the room, pass notes, and talk?" They know the answer. "See," I continue, "it is very important for martial arts students to control their bodies in every way. Do you understand?" "Yes sir."

I follow up by giving them an assignment to practice standing still for a couple of minutes every day. When teaching kids about control, remember to put a fun spin on it. You can illustrate the importance of sitting still with the game of Hide and Seek. Ask them if they would be successful at hiding if they couldn't sit still. This will help them understand.

It's not unusual for students to lose their self control in class. And when one kid acts silly, the rest follow suit. In these cases, if a verbal warning doesn't put them back on track, I ask the entire class to stand still and remain silent for a much longer time than usual. They are not allowed to move, laugh, talk, scratch, or even look around. I tell them that they have to stay that way until we have a room full of statues for ten seconds straight. If anyone moves or makes a sound, we start over. Sometimes this process takes several minutes but at the end, they are much more subdued – at least for a while.

If your child is acting like a wild hyena, try the same exercise. Make her sit completely still for a set period of time. If she even budges, make her start over. In the process of doing this exercise, you are helping her calm down by changing or interrupting her behavior pattern. Of course, this drill won't affect some kids and you may have to make some modifications. In extreme cases of "wild child," seek the professional help of a qualified martial arts school.

You can also calm a child down with physical exercise. This is an approach we often take with some excitable students. When all else fails, we wear them out with exercise or drills. It's a simple case of burning off the excess energy in a very positive way. Even the most difficult kids are much more manageable when they are worn out. Just remember, many self control issues are caused by too much pent-up energy. Children need a healthy way to relieve stress and aggression. Show them how to use this energy in constructive ways.

## MENTAL CONTROL

Self control is also the ability to resist breaking rules, over-eating, breaking promises, talking in class, getting out of line, wasting time, doodling instead of focusing, eating the wrong foods, playing a video game instead of doing their homework, talking back, or yelling in the house. As they grow older, self control will also help them resist peer pressures like smoking, drinking, taking drugs, and behaving certain ways while seeking the approval of the "cool" crowd.

As always, self control begins with parents. Don't temp kids to do something they shouldn't or don't need to do. For example, I had a friend over and he brought along his nineteen-month-old daughter. She was toddling around the house just enjoying herself, minding her own business and playing. Her dad was eating a cookie and offered her a piece. She said she didn't want any but he still offered the cookie several more times. "Are you sure you don't want a piece?" he said. I understand that we parents enjoy sharing things with our children, but this little girl didn't need that cookie. She was quite content without this treat which wasn't good for her in the first place.

Early in our son's life, my wife and I started the habit of not offering things to him that he didn't need. Many parents are quick to put a pacifier in their kid's mouth before he or she even cries or fusses for it. We decided that we wouldn't offer him one unless he pleaded for it. Soon he stopped asking for it all together. He lost interest in his pacifier by three months of age. Of course, some children will continue to use a pacifier and that's okay. This is just one example.

By giving kids things that we think they want but don't need just sets them up for self control issues later. They begin to think, that maybe they do want that. Soon my friend's daughter will think she wants that cookie, then another and another. Treats should be given as a reward or on special occasions, not as an everyday occurrence.

Remember to set a good example. Don't do anything in front of your children that you don't want them to do later. Again, monkey see, monkey do.

## EMOTIONAL CONTROL

Another critical aspect of self control is a child's emotional control. Learning to control emotions is an important part of good, long term mental health and affects physical well being as well. Emotional control is mandatory when a child possesses martial arts skills. I tell my students to keep their cool when someone is making them angry. Disagreements happen but we have to handle them smoothly. Disagreements can lead to arguments and arguments can lead to fights. When we control our tempers we not only avoid fights, we also avoid saying or doing things we may regret later. I use the following message to really drive home the idea that my students should refrain from arguing and fighting, even when pushed.

*Have you ever seen an eagle catch a fish before? Well, it is a spectacular event in more ways than one. As an eagle flies off to its perch to eat its food, it almost always faces a challenge even greater than catching its dinner. Smaller, less impressive birds known as "pest" birds actually attack the eagle. They make strikes at the eagle, try to take its dinner and even knock the eagle from the sky. As we all know, the eagle is much stronger and bigger than the pest birds and can easily use its huge talons to hurt the pest birds. But eagles also have a great deal of self control.*

*Instead of fighting those smaller birds, the eagle actually follows a different plan. The mighty eagle knows that it can fly much higher than any other bird. So, instead of fighting, it flies higher and higher until the pest birds can no longer keep up so they give up. Having nothing to prove to the pest birds, the great eagle soars way above them until it reaches its perch.*

### Follow-up Questions

1. Does the eagle have the ability to hurt the pest birds?

2. The eagle shows strength and flies higher than all of the pest birds. How can you show strength if someone is pestering you?

3. Can you be like an eagle and soar above pests?

### Message

This is how I follow up with my karate students: "As martial artists, we develop skills that we can use to defend ourselves against "pest" people. As good martial artists, we know we should not use our skills unless it's absolutely necessary. When someone is pestering us, either by calling us names, teasing us or even pushing us around, we have a choice to make. Do we use our skills and fight with them or do we act more like the great eagle and "rise" above them? On the rare occasion we're actually in danger, we may have to use our skills but it's important to determine when we are actually in danger and when we're just losing our temper. An Elite Martial Artist will know the difference and possess the self control to take the appropriate action." You can explain fight avoidance to your child using the eagle story even if she isn't in martial arts.

## ANGER MANAGEMENT

This is an appropriate time to teach kids about anger management. I encourage my students to take a "cool down" if they feel their tempers flaring. When someone is pushing us to our limits of self control, it's critical that we refrain from letting our temper control our actions. Inevitably, we will do or say something we will regret. I tell my students to walk away from the situation and take ten deep breaths. If their confrontation is of a physical nature, I tell them to put their open hands up instead of fists. The open hands let the other party know that they don't want to fight. At this point, the student should tell the other person that they are going to go cool down because they are not allowed to fight.

If you and your child get into an argument, encourage them to take a cool down. Don't say, "Go to Your Room and Think About What You Did!" Instead try this. "Son, I think we're getting a little too worked up right now and we need to take a cool down. You go to your room for ten minutes and I'll go to mine. When we feel better, we can continue our conversation." Parents have a responsibility to display self control and set a good example. At the same time, you don't want to encourage kids to "repress" their emotions. After cooling down they should have the freedom to express their feelings when they are upset with you. Teach them that it's okay for them to politely ask if they can go cool down. Do not, however, allow them to stomp off in a tantrum to get away from you.

Children need to learn that there are consequences, other than punishment, to losing their tempers. Teach them that they can hurt someone physically or emotionally with their anger. Let them know there's more to gain from anger management than just staying out of trouble. Often, there are feelings at stake that can have a long term effect on relationships. Use the following story to help make the point clear.

*Once there was a little boy who had a bad temper. His father gave him a bag of nails and told him that every time he lost his temper, he had to hammer a nail into the back of the fence. The first day, the boy drove 37 nails into the fence. Over the next few weeks, as he learned to control his anger, he hammered fewer and fewer nails. Along the way ,he discovered it was easier to hold his temper than to drive those nails into the fence. Finally the day came when the boy didn't lose his temper at all and his father suggested that he pull out one nail for every day he was able to hold his temper.*

*The days passed and the young boy finally told his father that all the nails were gone. The father took his son by the hand and led him to the fence. He said, "You have done well, my son, but look at the holes in the fence. The fence will never be the same. When you say things in anger, they leave a scar just like these holes."*

## Follow-up Questions

1. Do you think the fence will ever look as good as new?

2. When you say things in anger to someone, do you leave scars on their feelings?

3. Do you think it's hard to mend someone's feelings after you hurt them?

## Message

Explain to your child that a verbal wound can be as painful as a physical one. Encourage them to use caution with their words and actions when they're upset. Also ensure that they understand the concepts of verbal, physical, and emotional control.

Emphasize the importance of self control every chance you get. Kids will inevitably need reminders when they're arguing in the back seat of the car, making loud noises when you're on the phone or when they're talking back or interrupting.

Look for opportunities to add some fun to their lesson in self control. Ask about their favorite super hero or their favorite mentor. Then quiz them on how their hero would act in a given situation. Remind them that when they stand still and remain quiet, they are acting like a ninja and also improving their Hide and Seek skills. Present self control as a positive, not a negative.

## POINTS TO REMEMBER

- Encourage kids to practice self control by being still and quiet. Make it fun when you can.

- Explain the benefits of good self control.

- Don't let their tempers flare. Encourage cool down time.

- Tell them the story provided and ask follow-up questions.

- Be consistent.

- Be a good example.

- Follow through.

# 9

# DISCIPLINE

*"When the subject matter is discipline, remember the
following: words convey the messages; but
actions teach the lessons."*

TERRY W. ALDERMAN
*AUTHOR OF DISCIPLINE: THE TOTAL APPROACH*

As Character Coaches, one of our most important tasks is teaching and instilling discipline in our kids. Discipline is the ability to follow directions and orders from someone of authority. It's also the ability to follow rules. Kids need to understand both the meaning and the benefits of being disciplined. Explain that discipline keeps kids safe and happy and it encourages people to follow rules, which in turn promotes fairness. Disciplined children are much more likely to succeed in school, sports, and extracurricular activities since they're more likely to follow structure. Respect for structure plays an important role later in building and maintaining a successful career.

## YOU GET THE BEHAVIOR YOU EXPECT AND ACCEPT.

When it comes to human behavior, Character Coaches get what they expect and what they accept. Make a list of the behaviors you expect from your child at home, at school, and in extracurricular activities. Then explain those expectations to your child. Help them understand why you want it this way and the benefits of good disciplined behavior as well as the consequences if they don't meet your expectations. Dr. Terry Alderman says, "Since most children are concrete thinkers, they require concrete examples (actions), not abstract messages, promises, or threats." So be clear and concrete in your instructions and follow up with questions. Ask them about the consequences of talking too much in school, or not following the rules in a baseball game. Then let them tell you why they should be disciplined in these situations. Ask them if they understand everything you talk about. By taking this approach, you're treating your child with respect while including him or her in the rule making process. As a result, your child will be more likely to follow those rules.

If your child's behavior is sub-standard, don't be tempted to "let it slide." By "letting it slide," you're letting them get away with something. Even a small infraction can be bad because then kids start to push their boundaries. They will test you. If you accept a behavior because you don't feel like punishing them, then you can expect more of the same behavior. Do not accept sub-standard behavior.

## MAKE DISCIPLINE COOL.

You're more likely to achieve discipline in kids when they *want* to be disciplined. Make discipline a goal or a desire for them. The following story is one that I use to demonstrate the merits of discipline and why it is in their best interests to obtain it.

*One day a Naval ship was towing a much heavier ship in a rough sea, using a very large, heavy, metal cable for the towing. Suddenly, in the midst of the wind and spray, the officer in charge of the ship shouted a single command -"DOWN!" On the spot, the crew of the ship flung themselves to the deck. Just then, the cable pulling the other ship broke and whipped around like a snake. If any man on that ship had hesitated to obey the commanding officer, he would have been killed instantly!*

### Follow Up Questions

1. What would have happened to the crew if they had just ignored the officer's command?
2. What if they had doubted or second-guessed the officer's command?
3. What would have happened if the crew had questioned why the commanding officer yelled before they hit the deck?

## MESSAGE

I go on to tell my students: "This is a good example of why it's so important to listen to your parents, teachers or karate instructors. The men on the ship didn't understand what was happening. They couldn't see the cable breaking. However, the commanding officer did see it and steered his crew away from injury or even death. Sometimes, your parents, teachers and karate instructors may be telling you to do something, and you may not understand why. They can see something you can't see. That is why you should trust them and obey commands." Then I ask them the follow-up questions above. The kids always know the answers. I continue to explain that their parents, teachers and other authority figures just want them to be safe and happy. Then I ask, "Who knows more about life at this point, you or your parents?" They always answer, "Our parents!" "You don't always need to understand why your parents tell you to do something, so just do it. They know things that you don't know yet and they're only trying to help you. Does that make sense?" I always ask them. "Yes, Sir!" they reply.

Remember, if you fail to teach your kids to follow directions and obey rules now, they will only encounter more trouble later - adult trouble. Breaking rules can become a habit and the older they are the bigger the consequences. Don't let things slide. Give them boundaries and make sure you reinforce good behavior.

## POINTS TO REMEMBER

- Explain the definition and importance of discipline.
- Help them see discipline as a positive.
- Tell them the story provided and ask follow-up questions.
- Be consistent.
- Be a good example.
- Follow through.

# 10

# SELF DISCIPLINE

*"You must take personal responsibility.*
*You cannot change the circumstances, the seasons, or the*
*wind, but you can change yourself."*

**JIM ROHN**
*BEST SELLING AUTHOR*
*AND MOTIVATIONAL SPEAKER*

After my beginner students understand the importance of respect, discipline, and self control, I teach them about self discipline. It simply means having the ability to take care of your responsibilities without having to be told so, regardless of how you feel about it. I demonstrate self discipline by showing them where to put their hands when performing a kick. I explain that they must keep their hands up while kicking or their opponent can strike them in the face. They can also lose their balance. I explain that since they're beginners, I'll probably have to remind them every once in awhile about the position of their hands. After they learn the hands skill, from my constant reinforcement or disciplining, I expect them to do it on their own. I always ask, "Whose job is it to do your homework - yours or your Mom's? Will your Mom get a bad grade if you don't do your homework? Whose job is it to brush your teeth? Will your Dad get cavities and bad breath if you don't brush your teeth?" The answers are just as obvious to them as they are to me. Then I ask, "So whose job is it to keep your hands up when kicking? Am *I* going to lose *my* balance or get socked in the face if *you* don't put *your* hands up?" Next, I expand on the idea, "What if a stranger or a bully is trying to hurt you? Who's going to put your hands up then? I can't be there to put them up for you. Do you understand?" When teaching your kids, use other ways to build self discipline like looking both ways before crossing the street, setting their alarm clock, and catching the bus by themselves. Just be sure that they understand the concept and give as many examples as you can that relate to their day-to-day life.

### SELF DISCIPLINE IS A SIGN OF LEARNING AND GROWING.

If a student of mine fails to put his hands up when defending himself, yell when he kicks or recoil a punch, it tells me that he is not ready to learn more. If he doesn't have the self discipline to follow my instructions, then he can't make the next step forward. I ask, "How many hands do you have? Is that a lot of hands to manage? What if you were an octopus? Then you would have some trouble. Can you keep track of two toys? Of course you can. So if I see your hands flailing around or hanging down, it tells me you are not keeping track of what your hands are doing while you're kicking. Can you do a better job of keeping your hands in the right place?"

Self discipline is as critical for advancement in martial arts as it is in other areas of life. Good self discipline provides the motivation to practice their martial arts techniques at home, study for a test, practice the piano for fifteen minutes, practice their lines for the play, turn in their homework, or practice dribbling the ball—all without you, the parent, having to enforce it.

Self discipline separates the "little" kids from the "big" kids and the "big" kids from the "grown ups." I explain to my students that if they can complete tasks that are their responsibility, they will be treated more like adults. Every kid reaches a stage where they want to be treated like an adult. So ask them if they're ready and willing to practice the habits of being an adult.

Another method I use to get it through to kids is this. "Do you like it when people tell you what to do? If you don't, then make yourself do it before they can. Play a game with your parents. See if you can go ahead and do the task they want you to do, whether it's clearing the dinner table, or taking the trash out before they get a chance to tell you. That way, they don't have to 'boss' you around. It's really simple to do since you already know what needs to be done, so do it quickly. Does that make sense?" Explain this to your kids and make a game out of it. With enough practice, they'll have the discipline to do it on their own.

## PRIORITIZING

Adults without self discipline don't accomplish much. They are procrastinators and slackers. Lack of self discipline is why people lose jobs, businesses close down, fitness levels decrease, bankruptcies occur, and even relationships fail. Obviously, kids should get in the habit of taking care of their responsibilities without having someone around to tell them to do it. Start them early. Make sure they understand there are things that have to be done regardless of how we feel about doing them. Once they understand the importance of self discipline, help them learn how to get organized and prioritize chores, homework, social engagements, and so on. Organization puts them in control so they feel less overwhelmed and anxious. In his book, *Seven Habits of Highly Effective Teens,* Sean Covey describes prioritizers as people who "take a look at everything they have to do and then prioritize, making sure their first things get done first and their last things last. Because they have the simple, but powerful habit of planning ahead, they're usually on top of things." Kids don't intuitively know how to prioritize. Give them a short list of things they have to do and let them put their tasks in order of importance. Start simple and then build up. Ask them which is more important to do first - the homework assignment that is due tomorrow or the one that isn't due until Friday? Which chore should we tackle first? Picking up the toys in our room or changing the cat litter that is overflowing? After they understand, make it more complicated. For example, which one should we do first - put our dirty clothes in the laundry room first or begin reading the assigned chapter in our book for school? You can lead them by telling them that you're getting ready to run a load of laundry. Let them think about that for a minute. Then let them in on the fact that their baseball or karate uniform is dirty and they need it tomorrow. Be patient and maintain a teacher's tone of voice. This method teaches them to think ahead and plan accordingly.

### PEOPLE WITH SELF DISCIPLINE ARE LEADERS.

Kids love the idea of being a leader. If you don't believe me, play a game of "follow the leader." It doesn't take long to figure out which role the child wants to play. Explain to your child, "If you are good at telling yourself which actions you should take and those you shouldn't take, then you are becoming a leader. How can you motivate anyone else to do something if you can't motivate yourself? Get in the habit of telling yourself to do certain things so you'll have the skill to motivate others. You have to develop self discipline yourself before you can lead others."

### SELF DISCIPLINE CREATES FREEDOM.

Kids who consistently display self discipline and responsibility earn the right to be trusted. Trust means more freedom. Trust from parents can grant the freedom to go to a movie with their friends, go down the street on their own, go shopping with the girls, and more. Explain this to your kids. The more they make good decisions while you're around, the more you will trust them to make those same, good decisions when you're not with them. I like the following illustration to help them understand the importance of being a self-boss:

*Stanley went on a camping trip with his father over the weekend. They went deep into the forest miles away from civilization. While on the trip, Stanley's father taught him how to use a compass. The compass is the little navigational tool that tells him how to go from place to place. It shows him which way is North, South, East, and West. His father explained to him that before he could venture too far into the forest, he had to learn how to use the compass and he had to obey it. Until he learned to obey the compass, he had to stay within sight of the campsite so he wouldn't get lost. Once Stanley became obedient to both the compass and his father's guidance, he soon had the freedom to go wherever the compass took him.*

#### Follow-up Questions

1. What would happen if Stanley went into the middle of the forest before he knew how to use the compass?

2. What would happen if he knew how to use the compass but

just ignored it?

3. Which people in your life are like a compass to you?

**MESSAGE**

Parents and teachers serve as a compass for us. They do their best to steer us in the right direction. When we follow them and discipline ourselves to do the right things we eat properly, exercise regularly, go to school and learn, and refuse to take drugs or drink alcohol. We give ourselves the freedom to grow up into the best human beings we can possibly become. We also achieve our goals by having self discipline in our lives. Like Stanley, we must become obedient and discipline ourselves to take actions that we know are good for us. Without a steering wheel, a car is under no one's control, but it won't move very far before running into something. People's lives are the same. Freedom comes only when we use self discipline to steer our lives.

Be sure to remind your children on a regular basis that you'll allow them more freedom to do more fun things once you trust them to take appropriate actions without instructing them.

## RESPONSIBILITY

Today not nearly enough people take responsibility for themselves or their actions. It's why there are so many frivolous lawsuits, unnecessary abortions, and mounting bankruptcies. Virtually everything that happens to a person is due to a decision he or she made beforehand. People who don't understand this concept are the people who do nothing but blame and complain and get lost in the shuffle. Lou Holtz said, "The man who complains about the way the ball bounces is likely the one who dropped it." People like this are not ready to accept the fact that they're a product of the decisions they make. These people miss appointments, are late for classes, lose their belongings, sit on the side of the road because they don't maintain their car. Chances are their dog has heartworms.

We can set our kids up for success by teaching them to be responsible for themselves, their actions and their belongings. Let's start with their belongings. I attended an elementary school as a "teacher for the day" not long ago and I couldn't believe the volume of stuff I saw in the hallway. There were four large cafeteria tables lined up against the wall stacked three feet high with shoes, jackets, books, sweatshirts – you name it. There were even piles of clothes and toys on the floor underneath the tables. This was the school's Lost and Found with enough to clothe an entire third world country. This happens at my karate school too. Kids leave their sparring equipment, jackets, and, my favorite, their shoes in winter time. How do they get to their car with bare feet when it's 35 degrees out? How do their parents let them? Remind your kids often to keep their belongings *their* belongings. This is the first step to having a responsible child. Praise them when they do a good job keeping track of their stuff.

Give your kids the responsibility of managing important papers, appointments, and money. Let them carry the ticket from the box office to the theatre when you go to see a movie. Help them understand the importance of hanging on to that ticket. Don't pressure them but let them know that you're counting on them. Ask them to remind you about something (something you would remember anyway). I do this all the time. If I have an important announcement to make at the end of a class, I will tell one of the students at the beginning to remind me later about the announcement. They never fail me because they don't want to disappoint me. They feel cool because they are privy to information and they have a task that no one else has. Even if I remember on my own to make the announcement, I let them remind me anyway. I always thank them for remembering the announcement. Without them, I never would have remembered.

Through this exercise, I teach them how to store important information in a different area of their brain. I raise their confidence and boost their sense of responsibility. They know I count on them and they perform. If they receive enough of this reinforcement, they come to enjoy the feeling of being responsible.

It's never too early to teach kids to be responsible with their money. They should keep Tooth Fairy money, birthday money, and chore money all in a safe place. Teach them that responsibility of money involves saving it, sharing it, and spending it. Financial counselor Dave Ramsey suggests that kids have three safe places to keep money. They can use piggy banks, boxes, or envelopes. One is for saving, one for giving and one for spending. By separating their money, they're learning to do the same thing when they are older. Having money is a big responsibility. If you have it, you should share some of it. To keep it and make it grow, you must save some of it. And to feel the reward of earning it, they should to spend some of it.

The next level of responsibility can be a more substantial commitment like having a pet. Before taking this step, be sure you're committed to making your child responsible for his or her pet. Understand that you will have to do a lot of supervising. You'll have to take the dog out and clean up after it. It may keep you up at night. This is all part of owning a pet. Remember, we are teaching kids responsibility and they aren't very good at it yet. Although it's hard work for a family to adopt a new pet, the lessons learned are invaluable. You might want to start with an animal that's fairly self sufficient like a turtle or an older dog or cat from a shelter.

### POINTS TO REMEMBER

- Let kids know the tasks that are their responsibilities.
- Explain to them that these tasks must be performed despite how they feel about it.
- Tell them they will have more freedom if they demonstrate self discipline.
- Tell them Stanley's story and ask follow up questions.
- Be consistent.
- Be a good example.
- Follow through.

# FOCUS

*"If I have made any valuable discoveries, it has been owing
more to patient attention than to any other talent."*

**SIR ISAAC NEWTON**
*ENGLISH MATHEMATICIAN*

Focus is the ability to center your concentration on one thing at a
time. Without focus, you can't learn, and if you can't learn, you can't
grow. Focus is one of the biggest deficiencies we see these days in terms
of child rearing which is why there are so many new drugs for such
highly publicized "disorders" as Attention Deficit Disorder (ADD)
and Attention Deficit Hyperactivity Disorder (ADHD). When I was
growing up, I was very "hyper" and in fact, I still am. Did my parents
put me on drugs? No, they accepted the fact that I had a lot of energy
so they kept me busy with chores, sports, and martial arts. And they
tanned my hide, if needed.

## HYPERACTIVITY MAY BE A SIGN OF GENIUS.

Kids who are "hyper" and seemingly can't pay attention are made for
martial arts. Psychologists suggest that hyperactivity and lack of focus
are often signs of intelligence. There are legitimate cases of ADD that
probably do warrant medication, but it's likely that many of these kids
are just bored and are not getting the stimulation they need to stay
focused. I often find that I have children in the four to seven-year-old
class who begin to misbehave with wandering focus and lack of self
control. If I move this child to the older age group, more times than
not, their focus becomes laser sharp because the previous curriculum

was just too easy for them. The lessons weren't enough to hold their interest so they acted up out of boredom.

For a child to focus, they must first be interested. Kids don't have a difficult time focusing on their video games or favorite TV show. Parents and teachers have a responsibility to keep them interested in the task at hand. I tell them the following story to prove a point:

*John Jones was in New York City waiting for his flight to Boston. Having a few minutes to spare, he walked over to a scale that weighs people and tells a fortune. He stepped on, inserted a coin and out came his fortune. It read: "Your name is John Jones, you weigh 188 pounds, and you are going to catch the 2:20 flight to Boston." He was astounded because all of the information was correct.*

*He figured this must be a trick, so he stepped back on the scale, inserted another coin and out came his fortune. "Your name is still John Jones, you still weigh 188 pounds, and you are still going to catch the 2:20 flight to Boston." Now he was more puzzled than ever. Sensing a trick, he decided to "fool" whoever was responsible. He went into the men's room and changed clothes. Once again he stepped on the scale, inserted his coin and out came his fortune: "Your name is still John Jones, You still weigh 188 pounds—but you just missed the 2:20 flight to Boston.* [2]

### FOLLOW-UP QUESTIONS

1. Why did Mr. Jones miss his flight?

2. What would happen if you were up to bat and you looked up in the stands at your Mom and Dad when the pitcher threw the ball your way?

3. What would happen if you thought about your video game while you were in karate class?

4. What would happen if you day dreamed while your teacher discussed a new math problem?

### MESSAGE

Mr. Jones clearly missed his sole reason for being at the airport because he shifted his focus. If you shift your focus in a baseball game, at school, or karate class, you will miss the reason for being there. Just like Mr. Jones, you'll come for one reason and you'll miss it. You will miss the ball, or fail to learn the new lesson at school or the new skill in karate. Focus is a skill we learn. We have to train ourselves to always stay focused on the task at hand.

The good news is that focus is like a muscle. The more you exercise it, the stronger it gets. It's up to parents and teachers to motivate kids to exercise this "muscle." Just as we want them to exercise physically, we have to provide them with opportunities to strengthen their focus. At my school, we start with kicking a target. The next level of focus is kicking a moving target. At higher levels, students have to focus on an opponent who is trying to kick or punch them. They have to see these attacks coming and block them as well as spot openings to throw their offensive strikes. Kids learn focus in my program because they want to progress. Their reward is moving on to more interesting and challenging techniques when they demonstrate their ability to focus.

Look for activities, big or small, that allow your kids to practice concentrating. Simon Says is a great tool. Explain to them that they can win the game only if they really listen to your instructions. We all know there is a big difference between just hearing and listening. Make it clear that they can not just "hear" your instructions - they have to really listen to make the correct move. If they move without Simon saying so, remind them to carefully listen and try again. If they do well, praise them. Show them how proud you are that they are becoming more focused.

## LET THEM BE BORED!

It's okay for kids to be bored. Give them a chance to be alone with their own thoughts occasionally. The earlier they get comfortable with this, the better. Everything around us is about instant gratification. The slowest Internet connection should still amaze us, but it doesn't. We expect instant access to information from around the world. Video games have to be packed full of realistic stimulation or they're boring. Don't allow your kid to resort to their "Game Boy" every time they have to wait for something. Let them be bored! Conquering boredom is an important skill. They need to know how to think and visualize. They need to know how to use their own imaginations. I fear that imagination may soon to be on the endangered species list.

Imagination is one of the greatest gifts a child possesses. It keeps them occupied and it sparks creativity. As adults, imagination and creativity are essential to living the life you want. Ask any entrepreneur if they think imagination is important. Would we have ever gone to the moon without it? We wouldn't fly airplanes or drive cars if these machines weren't once part of someone's imagination? Bill Gates had an active imagination, so I'm able to write this book on one of his computer programs. What if scientists couldn't imagine finding cures for diseases? Allow your child the time to let their imaginations run wild. Remember how much fun you could have as a kid with a stick in the backyard? Most kids these days wouldn't know what to do without their TVs and video games. Take them away from the electronics and make them play outside. Encourage them to use their imaginations. As Albert Einstein said, "Imagination is everything. It is the preview of life's coming attractions."

## POINTS TO REMEMBER

- Focus, like a muscle, must be exercised to become stronger.
- Help them stay on task. It will take practice, especially if your child has lots of energy.
- Tell them the story provided and ask follow up questions.
- Be consistent.
- Be a good example.
- Follow through.

# PERSEVERANCE

*"By perseverance the snail reached the ark."*

CHARLES SPURGEON
*NINETEENTH CENTURY BRITISH MINISTER*

Perseverance is the unwillingness to give up when a task is challenging, in other words the refusal to quit. We teach our kids that anything worth doing is worth doing right. The more work involved, the greater the reward. While in pursuit of big rewards, kids will be faced with many opportunities to quit. So it's imperative to teach children that they shouldn't quit once they start something so they'll experience more success. Robert Strauss said it best when he observed, "Success is a little like wrestling a gorilla. You don't quit when you're tired - You quit when the gorilla is tired."

In the martial arts, we use a particular stance designed to strengthen the legs while we practice hand techniques. It is called the Horse Stance. Students spread their feet out twice the width of their shoulders and bend their knees as if riding on horseback. I tell the students that I can learn a lot about them just by watching them do this stance. I tell them that I can determine whether or not they're the kind of kid who gives up when the going gets tough. Legs become fatigued quickly in the Horse Stance, so it doesn't take me long to assess the kids' level of perseverance. If they straighten their knees into a more comfortable position after only a few seconds as a beginner or half a minute as a more advanced student, then I can tell that they might need perseverance coaching in not only their Horse Stance, but in all areas of their lives. They may not realize it, but they are giving up on the stance. Sometimes they consciously decide to straighten their knees. Other times, they give up without even realizing it. It makes me wonder how these kids read a book that is less than desirable, struggle with difficult math problems, or come back from behind in the last 100 meters of a race.

## PERSEVERANCE IS MENTAL TOUGHNESS.

Some kids have to learn the ability to persist. They don't start out intending to give up, and they don't necessarily want to give up, but they do anyway. That's why it's so important to explain the benefits of hanging in there and then teaching them how to become stronger mentally. If a child can't keep his knees bent in the horse stance, he won't gain the full benefit of the position. His legs will not become stronger. However, if he learns to keep his knees bent, he will build strong legs capable of better kicks and higher jumping. Perseverance is patience in action. The following fable is a great example of how we sometimes have to wait patiently with perseverance to see results.

*A particular species of Chinese bamboo has a rather difficult growing cycle. During the first year, a gardener can water and fertilize the plant but nothing happens. The second year a gardener can continue to water and fertilize it and still nothing happens. The third and fourth years, the gardener continues to water and fertilize it religiously with no apparent results. But sometime during the course of the fifth year, in a period of six weeks, the Chinese bamboo tree grows roughly ninety feet.*

### FOLLOW-UP QUESTIONS

- Does the bamboo plant grow ninety feet in six weeks or does it grow ninety feet in five years?
- Would you have the patience to continue caring for a pot of dirt for five years?
- Can you think of a time when you worked on something for a long time without seeing any results, but eventually it paid off?

### MESSAGE

In this example, we learn that results don't always appear immediately after we start working towards a goal. The bamboo obviously grew ninety feet in five years because the gardener applied water and fertilizer each year. Otherwise, there would be no Chinese bamboo tree. All of us have had those "Chinese Bamboo Tree" experiences. Help your child think of examples of when the reward for a task was delayed.

With my students, I use the example of doing Chinese splits. Students can stretch for months or even years without accomplishing the full splits but if they keep working, they will eventually master the splits. Another example is doing a difficult assignment in math, social studies or science. They might have to work at the assignment again and again without coming up with the correct answer. Once they finally get the answer, it often seems simple and obvious. They eventually come up with the answer not because they suddenly acquired intellectual brilliance but because they practiced perseverance.

It's vital that they develop a strong sense of perseverance early so the habit of working through challenges is ingrained in their heads. Later we will discuss goal setting in detail. For now, remember that a goal is anything that stretches you to do something you haven't already done or to become someone you've never been before. It's always challenging to grow as a person. Take the example of Thomas Edison who overcame many challenges and failures, but never gave up. Tell your kids this story.

## LEAD-IN QUESTIONS

1. Do you know who Thomas Edison is? Then explain his most famous invention - the light bulb.

2. How many times do you think he tried before he got it right? Let them make some guesses and then tell them "more than 10,000 times!"

*While being questioned by a young reporter about an invention he had been working on for a long time, Thomas Edison revealed one of the secrets of his greatness. The young reporter asked, "Mr.Edison, how does it feel to have failed 10,000 times in your present venture?" Edison replied, "Young man, since you are just getting started in life, I will give you a thought that should benefit you in the future. I have not failed at anything 10,000 times. I have successfully found 10,000 ways that will not work!"*

## MESSAGE

Edison estimated that he actually performed over 14,000 experiments in the process of inventing and perfecting the incandescent light. He discovered plenty of ways that wouldn't work, but he persevered until he found one way that would. He proved that the only difference between the "big shot" and the "little shot" is the big shot is simply a little shot that keeps shooting. This is why perseverance is so important. It's not easy for most kids to get straight A's. It's not easy to be the captain of the soccer team. It's not easy to achieve the goal of Black Belt. Later in life, it won't be easy to earn a college degree or receive promotions at work. All of these important steps are both challenging and rewarding. Henry Ford once said, "Failure is the opportunity to start over again more intelligently." With each setback your child experiences, be there to help them find the lesson to be learned.

A good way to develop your child's perseverance is by occasionally reminding him of its importance. When your child does something that requires him to "stick to it" and persevere, reward him for it. Let him know how proud you are. I do this on a regular basis when awarding students new belt ranks. After moving up through the ranks, they soon learn that accomplishing the difficult task is its own reward.

### INDOMITABLE SPIRIT

Indomitable spirit is akin to perseverance, but it has a little twist. Kids should understand that sometimes in life things aren't only difficult, they seem downright impossible and that's where having the spirit to persist comes in. "Life is unfair," said John F. Kennedy. My dad echoed that almost on a daily basis. Abraham Lincoln put it this way, "Success is going from failure to failure without losing enthusiasm."

Kids will often feel everything is stacked against them and sometimes it's true. Sometimes, other kids ridicule and bully them. These are the times when kids need to see that there is a light at the end of the tunnel. They have to show perseverance and reach deep inside themselves to find the spirit to keep going. I use one of my favorite parables to illustrate the point.

*One day a farmer's donkey fell down into a well. The animal cried piteously for hours while the farmer considered his options. Finally he decided the animal was old and the well should be covered up anyway. It just wasn't worth it to retrieve the donkey.*

*So he invited all of his neighbors to come over and help him. They all grabbed a shovel and began to shovel dirt into the well. The donkey realized his predicament and cried horribly. Then, to everyone's amazement, he quieted down. A few shovel loads later, the farmer looked down the well and was astonished by the sight he saw.*

*With every shovel of dirt that hit his back, the donkey shook it off and took a step up. As the farmer's neighbors continued to shovel dirt on top of the animal, he shook it off and took another step up. Soon, everyone was amazed when the donkey stepped up over the edge of the well and trotted off.*

### FOLLOW-UP QUESTIONS

1. What did the old donkey do when it realized it was being covered with dirt?

2. What would have happened if the donkey had given up and let the dirt pile up?

### MESSAGE

Life is going to shovel all kinds of dirt on you. The trick to "getting out of the well" is to shake it off and take a step up. Each of our troubles is a stepping stone. We can get out of the deepest wells life puts us in by not stopping and never giving up. Shake it off and take a step up. It is important to learn how to choose our battles. We have to understand that life is not always smooth and people aren't always nice. As hard as it can be, we have to learn to let some problems roll off our backs.

### POINTS TO REMEMBER

- Perseverance means that we never give up.
- Refusing to quit is the key to being successful.
- A Black Belt is just a white belt who never quit.
- Tell kids the Bamboo lesson and the Donkey story and ask follow-up questions.
- Be consistent.
- Be a good example.
- Follow through.

# 13

# INTEGRITY

*"When I do good, I feel good. When I do bad,
I feel bad. And that's my religion."*

**ABRAHAM LINCOLN**
*SIXTEENTH PRESIDENT OF THE UNITED STATES*

Put simply, integrity is matching your words with your actions. It means doing what you say you're going to do. It means being honest and true to your word. Integrity is doing the right thing, and doing it the right way. A person with integrity is always there when they say they are going to be there and they always do what they say they are going to do. In other words, you can count on a person with integrity. They are dependable. They have a working conscience. They always do the right thing even if it inconveniences them. Abraham Lincoln got his nickname, "Honest Abe," because he walked several miles back to a store to return only a couple of pennies that he was overpaid. You can count on someone with that kind of dedication to truthfulness for just about anything.

Someone lacking in integrity will lie, cheat, and steal. They rarely deliver on their promises. They are so self-absorbed that no one else's schedule or feelings matter. They cut corners and do things haphazardly. They are the ones who sweep things under the rug. They never give change back to a clerk if they were given too much. Listen to some of the statistics Bob Alexander provides in his book, *The Teacher Trap*. He said that according to a study by the Josephson Institute of Ethics, 71% of all high school students admit they cheated on an exam at least once in the past 12 months (45% said they did so two or more times). 93% lied to their parents in the past 12 months (79% said they did so two or more times) 78% lied to a teacher (58% two or more times); more than one in four (27%) said they would lie to get a job. 40% of males and 30% of females say they stole something from a store in the past 12 months. To me, these numbers are alarming and they demonstrate why it's so important to teach our kids honesty and how to match our words with our actions.

## HONESTY IS THE BEST POLICY.

Honesty has to start early. If you let kids get away with lying, cheating, or stealing, even if it's minor offenses, they will do it again. Very young children who have figured out this consequence and punishment thing will look you in the eye and lie to avoid punishment. You've seen it. They will lie even if they're in the right. They will pass the blame onto a sibling or friend without a flinch. They'll steal something from their brother and when the brother tells on him, what will the offender say? "Nuh, uh, he wasn't using it." It's amazing how little regard some youngsters have for the truth. Most of this is natural. Kids will do anything to avoid punishment. Sometimes they just want to see if they can get away with something. None of it is cute. You have to nip dishonesty in the bud. If kids don't grasp the importance of honesty early, they could be headed for expulsion from school or even jail later on.

When a child is in trouble with you, but tells the truth about what happened, be sure to let that child know how proud you are of them for being honest. You might even lessen the punishment a little just to prove the point that honesty is best. By the same token, if child is in trouble and lies, make the punishment more severe. Be sure to let them know why you adjusted the punishment For example, let's say that Betty stole money out of your purse or wallet, and she fesses up to it. Let her know that she is in big trouble for stealing. Her punishment would have been grounding for a month, for example, but since she was strong enough to tell the truth, you will take a week off the sentence. Don't give her too sweet of a deal, because she has to be properly punished for the offense. If she lies about it and you know better, increase the sentence a week. Adjusting the punishment and explaining why will promote honesty in the future.

### KEEPING THEIR WORD.

Make sure your children understand the meaning of keeping their word. This goes for promises and keeping harmless secrets. If they say they are going to start their homework when their favorite show is over, hold them to it. Learning to keep secrets comes in handy when you want your child to stay quite about siblings' birthday presents, for example. Be sure they understand when it's time to tell an adult about a secret that could be harmful. For example, they should always tell an adult if a sibling or friend is doing something that could be dangerous or unlawful. Also make it clear that they must not keep secrets from you that he or she makes with another adult. If another adult does or says something to your child that they say you shouldn't know about, it is seldom a good thing.

### STEALING FROM OTHERS
### IS STEALING FROM YOURSELF.

The issue of stealing is a tough one. It's a two-headed dragon. Stealing can be an adrenaline rush because the child acquires a new possession. Kids love excitement, and they love stuff. If there is something unguarded and they want it for themselves, why not? It could be something very small. For example, a student might "find" a pen under someone's desk at school and although they know full well who the owner is, they keep it anyway. If they get away with something this simple, why not take a step up and go for something bigger? Let kids know that things that are not theirs are not theirs and others' possessions are not up for grabs. When they find something, encourage them to try to find the rightful owners so they understand that it feels better to give back to someone than to take away from them.

If a child gets away with stealing or is not punished sufficiently, that child will do it again and again until someone catches them who is serious about the consequences of stealing. I have seen it too many times. They start small, for example, taking candy from a convenience store. The excitement of getting away with it leads them to try and find a bigger rush. Then they move up to stealing change and small belongings from people's cars at night. From there they might steal CDs, clothing and other items from stores that fit in their pants or shirt. If they get away with stealing enough, they may move on to bigger issues like grand theft auto or armed robbery.

Stealing can be like an addiction. Even if a child is punished for stealing, they are likely to do it again unless the punishment is severe enough. Don't take stealing lightly. It is a criminal act. Nip this one in the bud. When kids are little, be sure to punish them proportionately for the offense. Let them know that stealing from others is also stealing from themselves. By not working to obtain the items they are stealing, they are not growing as a person. If they do not experience earning possessions on their own through work, they will not become the person that they could be. We'll talk more about this in the Work Ethic section of the book, but if you make your child earn their possesions, they will be less likely to steal from others.

The following story encompasses all aspects of integrity. It shows the consequences of cutting corners, short cutting others, lying and stealing from others, and not remaining true to your word. It is an old tale about a building contractor who discovers what happens when the structural integrity of a person and a building are not up to standards.

*The owner of a construction company gave a job to one of his building contractors to build a house for an important client with a $300,000 budget. Since the contractor was a long-time faithful employee, the company owner also wanted to give him a gift for Christmas so he said that any money left over from the budget would be the contractor's. The contractor went to work. He wanted to build this house with as little money as possible so he could keep more for himself. Instead of using his normal crew, he hired new workers who were much less experienced and cost much less to hire. He also used the cheapest building materials. He cut every corner he could to save money. He even cut corners when it came to the foundation, roof, floors, ceilings, plumbing, and electricity. When the project was finished he was happy. Although the new house wasn't very sturdy, it looked good, and he came out $30,000 under budget.*

*The next day, the company owner called the contractor to the new house to look it over with him. The owner asked the contractor if he liked the design of the house. He asked him if he felt good about the build of the house and if it was a house he would live in. The contractor answered "yes" to all of the questions knowing he really didn't feel that way.*

*The company owner put his hand on the contractor's shoulder and said, "I'm glad you like this house because I had you build it for yourself. Merry Christmas! The house is yours!" The contractor couldn't believe it. He had just built a house for himself and his family that could collapse with just a light wind - a house with many, many potential problems.*

## FOLLOW UP QUESTIONS

1. What are some of the shortcuts the contractor took to save money?

2. For whom did he actually build the house?

3. Was he honest when he said he thought it was a nice house that he would live in?

4. By cutting corners, who did he end up hurting?

## MESSAGE

The contractor learned that cutting corners and not being honest only hurt himself. If he had actually built the house for another family, it would have hurt them. But luckily trying to shortcut and cheat the supposed owners of the house to benefit himself only proved harmful to him. The contractor will be reminded of this lesson every time it storms because he will wonder if his house is going to hold up. Every time he turns the plumbing and electricity on, he is going to wonder if it is going to work or not. He will worry that the roof will leak or the foundation will crumble. The structural integrity of the house is as unstable as his personal integrity. If his actions had matched his words, he would have a wonderful house for his family. Someone with integrity would have done the job right, even if it meant spending more money. Someone with integrity would have been able to say they would like to live in that house and mean it.

## POINTS TO REMEMBER

- Teach children early that honesty is the best policy. Reward them for honesty; punish them for dishonesty.

- Teach them when and when not to keep secrets.

- Teach them the consequences of stealing.

- Tell them the contractor's story and ask follow-up questions.

- Be consistent.

- Be a good example.

- Follow through.

# SELF IMAGE

*"Confidence is the self-assurance that you have reached a high level of proficiency with abilities that others can plainly see without verbal reminders from you."*

**HARRY KLAPHEKE**

*6TH DEGREE BLACK BELT, FORMER COO OF
A MULTI-MILLION DOLLAR COMPANY,
AUTHOR AND MY FATHER.*

Self image governs all behavior. The way a person feels about himself is the starting point for all other feelings. Everything anyone does or says can be traced back to self image. If someone has low self esteem, lack of confidence, or inadequate self respect, that person's life will be a struggle, marked by a lack of joy and an abundance of self-doubt.

We have all known someone who has low self esteem. These are the extremely shy, the complainers, the paranoid, those who possess negative attitudes and the easily offended. They tend to take everything personally. They don't have the confidence to pursue worthwhile goals or to even establish goals for that matter. They have a fear of failure. They give up when the going gets tough. Sometimes they give up just because they think the going is going to get tough. Many times they don't even get going at all. Many are shy. Some are attention seekers and they can be major league show-offs. They brag, use offensive language, and bully others - anything to get attention. Someone with a low self image assigns themselves value with their belongings. Many people do this with the car they drive, the neighborhood they live in, and the clothes they wear.

People with a low self image will do anything to fit in. They act like someone they are not to be like other people. They have no identity.

They hang out with "cool" crowds and people who are often not cool at all. They are extremely susceptible to drug and alcohol abuse. They are both victimizers and victims – often allowing people to bully or abuse them. This abuse only makes their self image worse.

People with a low self image are not bad people. They are just people who have lacked the support structure in their lives necessary to fill them with confidence. Some cases are due to abusive parents or authority figures. In many cases, their parenting was loving and kind, but there was just something missing. We have the opportunity to give our little people a healthy self image. Kids who feel good about themselves can potentially move the world and lead lives of significance and happiness. It all starts with the notions that we as Character Coaches put in their heads.

## LOVE

The most important ingredient for a healthy self image is love. Just showing your kids that you love them can raise their self worth. They feel more valuable if they know that you love them unconditionally and that you love them more than your job, your house, or your car. Your children need to know that you love them for who they are, not the things they do or the things they possess. Constantly tell them you love them. Make sure you give them plenty of hugs. As teachers and other professional Character Coaches, we can simply pat them on the shoulder or praise them verbally. Just listening to them means so much to children. Let kids know that you are there for them if they need you. Show them your pride in them. Speak highly of them privately and publicly. Make sure they know you are proud of them, no matter what they do or have. Don't compare them to other kids. Don't even compare them to yourself when you were their age. They are their own very unique selves.

## PRAISE

Praise is a very powerful tool for raising a child's self esteem. Every chance you get, shower them with praise. Starting as infants, children are making accomplishments that may seem trivial to us but they are huge to them. For each new accomplishment, have a small celebration by praising them immediately after the accomplishment or positive action.

The longer you wait to praise them, the less the impact. Be specific when you praise. I tell kids precisely the aspects I like most about their praiseworthy behavior. Being specific also shows them that you are not just flattering them. Never flatter kids. They can see right through insincerity. Praise them often to turn their good actions into lifelong habits.

When teaching or correcting children, use the principle of P.C.P. or Praise, Correct, Praise as mentioned in the Discipline Chapter in Part I. This way, you will ensure that they are learning and growing in a way that will boost their self esteem.

## GOALS

Help children set realistic, short term goals. These goals should be small and attainable in a very short period of time without a great deal of effort. If the goals are too hard or they have to wait too long to feel the victory of the goal, they may give up. These small goals can be steps towards a bigger goal. The point is that they are feeling victory as often as possible. Nothing raises self esteem like accomplishment. The more private victories they have, the more confidence they will have to pursue more public victories.

## POSITIVE MENTAL ATTITUDE

Shaping a positive mental attitude in children is essential for a healthy self image. This means teaching them to monitor the thoughts in their heads, particularly short-sighted beliefs. Control the messages that they hear from the media and their peers. We must teach them that what ever they think, they're right. For example, if one of my students thinks he can't perform a cartwheel, he's right – he can't. If he thinks he can do a cartwheel, he's right – he can. If he tells himself something, his mind will find reasons why he can or cannot do it. This is the power of positive and negative thinking and the reason we must teach our kids to think positively.

I use a great story Zig Ziglar calls "From Dunce to Genius." It sums up the whole idea of self image. This story is a good message because it shows the effects that a Character Coach's words can make, as well as the impact that a child's self-talk makes.

*When Victor Seribriakoff was fifteen, his teacher told him that he would never finish school and that he should drop out and get a job. Victor took the teacher's advice and dropped out of school. For the next seventeen years, he did a variety of odd jobs. People told him that he wasn't smart and he acted like it. When he was thirty two years old, an amazing thing happened. While applying for a job, an evaluation revealed that he was actually a genius with an IQ of 161. Guess what? Seemingly overnight, he started acting like a genius. Since that time, he has written books, created several inventions and become a successful businessman.*[2]

## FOLLOW UP QUESTIONS

1. When Victor dropped out of school, was he as dumb as his teacher thought?

2. How did he act when people told him he was dumb?

3. What did he become when he acted dumb?

4. How did Victor act when he found out he was a genius?

5. What did he become when he acted like a genius?

## MESSAGE

To paraphrase Mr. Ziglar's message, Victor's story makes you wonder how many geniuses we have walking around acting like dunces because somebody told them that they were dumb or inadequate. Obviously, Victor did not suddenly acquire a tremendous amount of additional knowledge all at once. He was already very smart with innate intelligence. However, he did suddenly acquire a tremendous amount of self worth. When Victor saw himself as a genius, he became more effective and more productive. When he saw himself differently, he started acting differently. He started expecting and getting different results. Victor's story shows us that self perception is self destiny – the way a person thinks about himself will determine the type of person he will become.

## POSITIVE SELF TALK

As Character Coaches, we must be careful about things we say to kids because they will take it to heart. We must also be careful about monitoring our kids' self talk. We should encourage their use of self affirmations instead of self-limiting beliefs. I tell my students I will not allow them to use "Four Letter Words," especially the ugliest one – CAN'T. The word "can't" is the most powerful negative word someone can say. Once people hear "can't" they go on a mental rampage trying to find all of the reasons why they can't do something. Luckily on the flip side, the most powerful phrases someone can say to himself are "I CAN," "I MUST," or, "I WILL!" Remember, whatever your child tells himself, he's right. Be sure to take time to explore your child's self talk and help them make it positive.

### POINTS TO REMEMBER

- Children won't feel like they are worth much unless you show them how much they are worth to you.

- Always praise them. Parental approval is one of the most powerful confidence boosters for kids.

- A sense of accomplishment is a self esteem vitamin.

- Having a positive mental attitude and positive self talk are crucial for a healthy self image.

- Tell them Victor's story provided and ask follow up questions.

- Be consistent.

- Be a good example.

- Follow through.

# HUMILITY

*"Only a life lived in the service of others is worth living"*

**ALBERT EINSTEIN**
*NOBEL PRIZE WINNER*

As children who are blessed to have a Character Coach like you improve their life skills, it is important that they understand humility. If you are consistent with all of the principles in this book and you follow through, the kids under your guidance will become so great that their heads may grow to a disproportionate size. We have to keep their egos in check. It is important that we make them understand that no matter how high we go in life, we are still servants to others which means we always put other people first. Teach kids to resist trying to make themselves look better than they are. That means no judging, no bragging, no showing off, no putting others down, no jealousy of others' accomplishments, and certainly, no turning their noses up. We have all seen these types of people and we don't particularly care to have them around for very long.

## CONFIDENCE VS. CONCEIT

There is a delicate balance between pride in accomplishments and boasting. Children should be happy about their accomplishments and celebrate them. That is how they raise their self esteem. Humility is not a lack of confidence. It's just the opposite. Humility is having enough confidence to know there is no need to boast. There is no need to put others down in order to feel bigger. Kids can talk positively about themselves but there is a line that shouldn't be crossed. A little showing off is okay but rubbing it in someone's face is not okay. Being excited about an accomplishment is different than proving to others that you are awesome.

It's natural for kids to be jealous of other kids' accomplishments because the spotlight is not on them and their confidence may be under attack. Confident kids who are humble will congratulate others and celebrate their victories with them. We have to let children know that just because someone else has the spotlight, it doesn't mean that there isn't some left for them. Many people can't celebrate others' successes because they feel that it may take some of the proverbial pie away from them. Let kids know that there is plenty of pie to go around.

## JUDGING OTHERS

Passing judgment is also a sign that we think we are better than someone else. It is not only wrong to judge, but your judgment is often wrong. The following story illustrates why we shouldn't judge people before we really know who they are.

*Years ago, a 10-year-old boy approached the counter of a soda shop and climbed up on a stool. "What does an ice cream sundae cost?" he asked the waitress. "Fifty cents," she answered. The boy reached deep in his pockets and pulled out an assortment of change, counting it carefully as the waitress grew impatient. She had "bigger" customers to wait on. "Well, how much would just plain ice cream be?" the boy asked. The waitress responded with noticeable irritation in her voice, "Thirty-five cents." Again, the boy slowly counted his money. "May I have some plain ice cream in a dish then, please?" He gave the waitress the correct amount, and she brought him the ice cream.*

*Later, the waitress returned to clear the boy's dish, and when she picked it up, she felt a lump in her throat. There on the counter the boy had left two nickels and five pennies. She realized that he had had enough money for the sundae, but sacrificed it so he could leave her a tip.*[2]

### Follow Up Questions

1. How much money did the boy have?

2. How much was the plain ice cream?

3. How much was the ice cream sundae?

4. Why did he order the plain ice cream instead of what he really wanted?

5. How do you think the waitress felt after she judged the little boy and found out that he was actually being nice to her?

## MESSAGE

Before passing judgment, first treat others with courtesy, dignity and respect. Adopt more of a service attitude and abandon the thought that you are "better" than anyone else. An example I use in my karate class is that of rank. When it's time to spar, the higher ranking, more experienced children have a decision to make when they are paired up with newer or smaller students. Is this a time to show the newer student how awesome they are and beat them down with some fancy techniques, or is it time to be a teacher and help them? They all know the answer to this question. I have made it very clear that these are perfect situations for practicing their humility and "serving-others" attitude.

Kids don't need to prove anything to anyone. Their actions speak louder than their words. Arrogant kids brag and judge. Humble kids are quietly great and serve others.

## POINTS TO REMEMBER

- Humility is not a lack of confidence.
- Humility is having enough confidence so there's no need to boast.
- Teach children to celebrate the victories of others.
- Don't let them judge others and don't do it yourself.
- Leaders serve others.
- Tell them the ice cream story provided and ask follow up questions.
- Be consistent.
- Be a good example.
- Follow through.

# PART III

## SKILLS
## FOR
## SUCCESS

# 16

# GOAL SETTING

*"Without goals, individuals just wander through life. They stumble along, never knowing where they are going, so they never get anywhere."*

**DAVID J. SWARTZ, PH.D.**
*PRESIDENT OF CREATIVE*
*EDUCATIONAL SERVICES, INC.*

One of the critical skills for success is goal setting. For thousands of years, martial arts have used a system of goals to help students achieve the level of Black Belt - the end goal that serious martial arts students strive for when they practice martial arts. No student has a goal of becoming a blue belt and quitting. The goal system of martial arts is designed to break down the daunting task of learning and perfecting the thousands of techniques required to reach Black Belt status. If martial arts teachers showed students all of the required skills simultaneously, those students would never pursue the goal of Black Belt because it would seem impossible. Instead, we break down all of the requirements into belt levels—steps towards achieving Black Belt. Students learn and perfect chunks of the material. Each month, we evaluate them and award them an approval stripe on their belt. Every three months, students graduate to a new belt color. By breaking the process into steps, we make the goal of Black Belt seem much more realistic. With each advancement, the students' confidence increases and their interest in working towards the next advancement and ultimately their Black Belt is renewed.

Working towards any worthwhile goal should be approached the same way. These are the steps to take:

1. First, you need to establish a goal and a timetable for achieving that goal. We let the kids know that the goal at our school is achieving Black Belt. We constantly remind them of this during class.
2. You have to make realistic plans for reaching your goal and follow through on them consistently. At our school, students have scheduled graduations recognizing advancement to their next belt as well as a class schedule to follow.
3. Identify a mentor who can aid and motivate you. My staff of instructors and myself are mentors for my students. Even a higher ranking student can be a mentor.
4. Relentlessly pursue the necessary steps or actions toward achieving your goal. Going to class consistently and practicing at home are steps that a martial artists must take to progress.
5. Reflect on your progress to ensure that you are still on the right track. Are your skills better than they were when you first started? Are they better than they were a month ago? Are they better than they were yesterday? If not, find a solution or another approach. If so, continue with that action.

One way to help your child understand how goal setting works is by using the following example: I like to ask my students if they go anywhere for vacation during their summer break. I then ask them how their parents plan for the trip. "Do your mom and dad just tell you to get in the car and start driving without a destination in mind? Or do they decide where they want to go and make plans for how to get there, how much to pack, how much money to take, and what the family will do when they get there?" This is an easy analogy to use to teach your child the value of goal setting.

Go through the steps with them.

1. "Let's decide where we want to go. Let's say Disney World. What's the date we intend to arrive there?"
2. "What is the next thing we will need to reach our destination? A map or directions."
3. "Who could we call about advice on the drive there? Uncle Charlie just went there last month. He could tell us the fastest way to go. He could tell us about any detours or pitfalls we might encounter. Since he's been there before, he could help make our journey a little easier.

We still have to make the journey ourselves, but he can help."
4. "What would happen if we didn't pay attention to Uncle Charlie's advice or the map? What if we decided to turn a different way and just be adventurous and go for it on our own? Would we reach our destination by the time we decided? Most likely not. So we have to follow the plan consistently."
5. "Have we driven far enough each day to ensure we get to Disney World by the date we planned?"

To make sure kids understand the process of goal setting, come up with an example goal. Ask your child the steps they can take to earn an "A" in math on the next report card. The steps would be:

1. Decide that an A is the desired target.
2. Encourage them to tell you a plan. Steps like studying an extra hour a day and paying better attention are good examples.
3. Ask them who could help. Possibilities are a tutor, the teacher, a mathematically inclined parent or even a student who has already attained the goal of an A. Also inquire about their study habits.
4. Can they study 1/2 hour one night, skip studying all together the next night and then study a full hour the next? No, they have to be consistent.
5. Are their grades getting better with each quiz? If not, they need to adjust their plan. If so, they should continue with their actions.

Allow your child to make big goals. If they set a goal of getting straight A's when they have a C average, make sure they understand that this is a big undertaking that will require hours of dedicated work. Then tell them that you believe in them and that you are there to help. Even if they fall short of getting all A's, at the very least they will bring their grades up.

The bigger the goal, the bigger the result. Big goals are also more difficult to obtain and difficulty can lead to failure. Let kids know this is going to be the case. Don't let them think that achieving goals is going to be easy so they won't be surprised and disappointed when setbacks occur. Remind them about Thomas Edison who "failed" more than 10,000 times before creating a light bulb.

Setting and reaching goals are important steps in building character for kids. Every time they reach a new goal, they become different people. If they were C students and their goal was to become an A student, they would have to change many things about themselves, including their study habits, their attention to detail, and their focus in the classroom. They would have to become different people. I explain this to my students concerning their belt ranks. When they achieve a new belt, they are not just receiving that belt - they are *becoming* that belt. Consequently, a Black Belt is something that they become, not something that they have. Help your child set worthwhile goals that stretch them and change them for the better into a new, updated version of themselves.

### POINTS TO REMEMBER

- Teach your children the value of goal setting.
- Teach them the steps involved.
- Remember the most important part of achieving goals is the personal growth they experience in the process. Help kids set worthwhile goals that will stretch them and change them for the better.
- Let them know that it is okay to fail but it is not okay to quit.
- Be consistent.
- Be a good example.
- Follow through.

# 17

# WORK ETHIC

*"If people only knew how hard I work to gain my mastery,*
*it wouldn't seem so wonderful at all."*

**MICHELANGELO BUONARROTI**

*ITALIAN RENAISSANCE ARTIST*

The more technologically advanced our society becomes, the lazier we become as a species. Technology is great, but you can never replace good old-fashioned hard work. Work is necessary to stay fit, obtain good grades, win the baseball game or accomplish any goal for that matter. The lack of good old-fashioned work is driving many people in our culture to poverty. People are geared towards instant gratification – the reason why "get rich quick" schemes and diet pills are so successful for those selling them. Everyone wants the best of everything right now without working for it. They want something for nothing. Tell your kids the following story about getting something for nothing.

*A number of years ago, some hogs escaped in a remote area of the Smoky Mountains. Over a period of several generations, these hogs became wilder and wilder until they were a menace to anyone who crossed their paths. A number of skilled hunters tried to locate and kill them but the hogs were able to elude the efforts of the best hunters in the area.*

*One day an old man, leading a small donkey pulling a cart, came into the village closest to the habitat of these wild hogs. The cart was loaded with lumber and grain. The local citizens were curious about the man's destination and his plans. He told them he had "come to catch those wild hogs." They scoffed because no one believed the old man could accomplish a goal that had eluded the local hunters.*

*But, two months later, the old man returned to the village and told the citizens the hogs were trapped in a pen near the top of the mountain. Then he explained how he caught them. "First thing I did was find the spot where the hogs came to eat. Then I baited the trap by puttin' a little grain right in the middle of the clearin'. Curiosity finally got to 'em and the old boar that led 'em started sniffin' around. When he took the first bite, the others joined in and I knew right then I had 'em.*

*Next day, I put some more grain out there and laid one plank a few feet away. That plank kinda spooked 'em, but that 'free lunch' had powerful appeal, so it wasn't long before they were back eatin'. Those hogs didn't know it but they were mine already. All I had to do was add a couple of boards each day by the grain until I had everything I needed for my trap. Then I dug a hole and put up my first corner post. Every time I added somethin', they'd stay away a spell but finally they'd come back to get somethin' for nothin.' When the pen was built and the trap door was ready, the habit of gettin' what they wanted without working for it drove 'em right into the pen and I sprang the trap. It was real easy after I got 'em comin' for the free lunch." [2]*

The habit of getting something for nothing spoils and shelters kids which makes the "real world" much harder on them. I always tell my students that they aren't going to receive their belts from me just because they are cute or because they ask for it. They have to earn it by working for it. I also tell them that they should earn their keep at home as well. They don't have any money to pay rent but they do have other forms of "currency." They should clean up after themselves, do their assigned chores and be respectful and helpful. Dave Ramsey, national talk show host, best selling author, and financial counselor says to "put kids on a commission schedule. Don't give them an allowance. They should only get paid for what they do." Children should have chores that are a given. These are earn-your-keep chores. They should have separate chores they can perform to earn money which helps kids understand that money comes from work. It doesn't come from looking cute, from being nice, from a money fairy and certainly not their parents. (You'll thank me for this one when it's time for them to leave the nest). By giving them an unearned allowance, you could be setting them up for financial failure later. They will expect the world to provide for them. If the world does not send them a check, they will expect the lottery to make things right. If that doesn't happen, they will be back at mom and dad's house. In his book, *Financial Peace,* Dave Ramsey says that "reports from the U.S. Census Bureau say that 59 percent of men from ages eighteen to twenty-five live with their parents. The same Census Bureau says that 48 percent of ladies from ages eighteen to twenty-five are also at home." He and I agree that there are some cases of emergencies but for the most part this rebound back to the nest is due to a poor work ethic. It is up to us as Character Coaches to make sure that kids start working as soon as possible. Again, please don't hear messages I am not saying. I'm not talking about child labor. I'm talking about earning their keep at your house, so they can keep their own house later.

## POINTS TO REMEMBER

- We live in a world where you can't receive something without working for it.
- Teach your children the value of work.
- Put children on a commission schedule for their chores.
- Teach them to earn their keep at home now so they can earn their keep later on their teams, in school, at work and even in their marriage.
- Be consistent.
- Be a good example.
- Follow through.

# 18

# ACTING AS IF

*"One of the great strategies for success is to act as if you are already where you want to be."*

**JACK CANFIELD**

*CO-AUTHOR OF CHICKEN SOUP
FOR THE SOUL*

We always reiterate to our students that they must strive for Black Belt Excellence which means acting as if they are already Black Belts. They must behave like a Black Belt would, whether they are in school, home, church, their friend's house, or at the karate school. Students must get into the habit of acting like a Black Belt early so their decisions and actions are congruent with those of a Black Belt the day they are awarded that rank. They must practice hundreds of physical techniques thousands of times before they are worthy of Black Belt status. The same is true of their behavior and attitude. Even when a student can perform physically at the Black Belt level, this does not necessarily grant them the right to wear a Black Belt. Any martial arts instructor would agree with me that a kid who is good at martial arts but does not have the Black Belt attitude can be dangerous.

In order to achieve goals, we must understand the importance of acting as if we have already met our goals. When students behave like a Black Belt, others will treat them like a Black Belt. This respect they experience will create a feeling of confidence fueling their subconscious mind to attract people who can help them achieve their goal. This confidence will also guide their decisions at a subconscious level and keep them motivated.

This approach can and should be used for reaching any goal. I tell kids that if they want to be a professional baseball player, they should act like one. When they are at practice or in a game, they should behave just as a pro would (except maybe the spitting part). They shouldn't be goofing off in the outfield and day-dreaming. They should be focused on the game. I encourage them to watch professional games and study the players' action. Then I tell them to try to emulate these actions every chance they get. (It wouldn't hurt if you asked them to autograph a ball for you!)

If your child wants to be a straight A student then she should act like one. She should sit up in her desk at school, stay focused on the teacher and attempt to answer questions. She should adopt the same study habits as a straight A student. She should try her best to emulate the ways of someone who already has achieved the goal she wants.

Like your kids, it is important for you to act as if you are the Character Coach that you want to be. Be sure to always show your children that you too can live by the principles in this book. Even if you struggle with some of the principles, don't let your children know. Act as if you are an expert Character Coach and you will soon become one. You are the biggest influence in your kids' lives. Strive to become the best person that you can be so your kids have good footsteps to follow. Because, believe me, they will follow your every footstep, good or bad.

**POINTS TO REMEMBER**

- Encourage your children to act like they are the person they want to become.
- Treat them as if they have already achieved their goal.
- Make sure you act as if you are the best Character Coach you can be.
- Your kids will follow in your footsteps.
- Be consistent.
- Be a good example.
- Follow through.

## CONCLUSION

We all want the best for our kids. We want them to be happy, healthy, and safe. We want them to succeed in school, sports, music, art, and hobbies. We want them to make good friends and have fun. We want them to have all of the positive experiences that are possible in their lives. We want our kids to grow up to be successful - in college, their careers, their finances and their relationships with family and friends. We want them to go on to become positive Character Coaches themselves.

Principles like Respect, Humility, Self Image, and Integrity are necessary for building and maintaining good relationships with friends, family, classmates, teammates, siblings, and later, their spouses, co-workers, clients and children. Discipline, Self Control, Focus, Perseverance, and Work Ethic are essential in setting and obtaining goals including high performance in school, career, finances, and health.

We can make this happen for our kids. Ultimately it's up to us. As Character Coaches, we have the opportunity to make a positive impact on our kids and our community. It is completely in our hands. We are like sculptors who have the power to mold our children into masterpieces. We have to establish structure for our kids and condition them to form habits that are necessary for success.

Remember, you can't give someone something that you don't already possess. To be a positive role model you must learn and practice the principles in this book. The principles must become a part of you. It is not enough to throw around words like "integrity" and "discipline" like they are just clichés. Words like these must be converted into actions which will become habits that will shape our character and ultimately our destiny. Don't just memorize the principles in this book and their meanings. Make them a part of yourself. Only then can you pass these positive traits on to the children under your influence.

Reread this book several times until all of the principles are clear to you. Know them backwards and forwards. Practice them. Watch other Character Coaches and how they behave and interact with their children. Read other books and do research. Practice being a good role model. Put time and energy into it because this is the most important task of your life. Raising kids is a pass/fail course so you must put more effort into being a Character Coach than you ever have at work or school. Being the best Character Coach you can be is its own reward. You will not only improve the lives of all of the children in your life but you will enjoy them more too.

You are a great Character Coach. Your kids are lucky to have you. Finally, be consistent. Be a good example. Follow through. Good luck.

## NOTES

*Success-One Day at a Time*, by John C. Maxwell. Nashville, TN: Maxwell Motivation, 2000.

Adapted from Zig Ziglar's I CAN Character Curriculum manufactured and distributed by Bob Alexander and The Alexander Resource Group.

## SUGGESTED READING

*Raising Positive Kids in a Negative World*, by Zig Ziglar. Nashville, TN: Zig Ziglar, 1979

*Seven Habits of Highly Effective Teens*, by Sean Covey. New York, NY: Fireside, 1998

*Financial Peace*, by Dave Ramsey. New York, New York: Penguin Group, 2003

*Million Dollar Habits*, by Brian Tracy. Canada: Entrepreneur Media Inc., 2004

*Success-One Day at a Time*, by John C. Maxwell. Nashville, TN: Maxwell Motivation, 2000

*The Teacher Trap*, by Bob Alexander. Macon, Georgia: The Alexander Resource Group. 2002

*The Success Principles*, by Jack Canfield. New York, NY: Harper Collins, 2005

*Black Belt Leadership*, by Harry C. Klapheke. Nashville, TN: Wolf Pack Publishing, 2000

*How to Win Friends and Influence People*, by Dale Carnegie. New York, NY: Pocket Books. 1936

*Principle Centered Leadership*, by Stephen R. Covey. New York, NY: Free Press. 1990

*The Magic of Thinking Big*, by David J. Schwartz. New York, NY: Simon & Schuster, 1987

CONTACT INFORMATION:

## Daniel Klapheke

## Elite Martial Arts of Brentwood Inc.
6940 Moores Ln.
Brentwood, TN 37027

**elitemartialarts.org**
**615-661-5595**

ISBN 142512011-3

9 781425 120115